THE MACMILLAN SHAKESPEARE
GENERAL EDITOR: PETER HOLLINDALE
Senior Lecturer in English and Education, University of York

ADVISORY EDITOR: PHILIP BROCKBANK
Professor of English and Director of the Shakespeare
Institute, University of Birmingham

ROMEO AND JULIET

THE MACMILLAN SHAKESPEARE

ROMEO AND JULIET

Edited by
James Gibson
Principal Lecturer in English,
Christ Church College, Canterbury

Nelson

Thomas Nelson and Sons Ltd
Nelson House   Mayfield Road
Walton-on-Thames   Surrey
KT12 5PL   UK

51 York Place
Edinburgh
EH1 3JD   UK

Thomas Nelson (Hong Kong) Ltd
Toppan Building 10/F
22A Westlands Road
Quarry Bay   Hong Kong

Thomas Nelson Australia
102 Dodds Street
South Melbourne
Victoria 3205   Australia

Nelson Canada
1120 Birchmount Road
Scarborough   Ontario
M1K 5G4   Canada

© Introduction and Notes, James Gibson 1974

First published by Macmillan Education Ltd 1974
ISBN 0-333-14929-7

This edition published by Thomas Nelson and Sons Ltd 1992

ISBN 0-17-432412-X
NPN 9 8 7 6 5 4 3 2

Printed in Hong Kong.

CONTENTS

CONTENTS

INTRODUCTION

THE DATE AND TEXT

There is no external evidence which will help to date *Romeo and Juliet*, but on the internal evidence of its style it is generally agreed that it was written about 1595. Shakespeare was then aged thirty-one and had been writing plays since about 1590. He was to continue writing until about 1612, and this makes *Romeo and Juliet* one of his earlier plays, written a quarter of the way through his career. There are many indications that this is the play of a comparatively young man, not least the obvious sympathy felt for the young as they struggle to escape from the morass of hatred created by their elders. Among the characteristics of style which help to date it are its youthful exuberance, its interest in verbal ingenuity and experiment, and an intense lyricism which associates it with *A Midsummer Night's Dream* and *Richard II* which we know were written about 1595. This is certainly not the work of a beginner, and by this time Shakespeare would have had eight or nine plays behind him, but it lacks some of the tautness, muscularity and depth of his more mature work. It has a particularly close link with *A Midsummer Night's Dream* as both plays are concerned with the nature of love – we remember Lysander's 'The course of true love never did run smooth', and his description of love as 'Swift as a shadow, short as any dream, / Brief as the lightning . . .' – and there are verbal echoes such as those we find in the Nurse's laughable lament over the supposedly dead Juliet which is so reminiscent of the ludicrous language used by Bottom when he acts the part of Pyramus.

We know that *Romeo and Juliet* must have been written by 1597 because it was first published in that year with the title, *An Excellent conceited Tragedie of Romeo and Juliet. As it hath been often (with great applause) plaid publiquely, by the right Honourable the L. of Hunsdon his Servants*. This edition is known as the First Quarto (Q1). Only about half of Shakespeare's plays were published in his lifetime, and it was not until seven years after his death that, in 1623, thirty-six of his plays were collected together by two of his fellow-actors and published in the First Folio (F1). The 1597 publication of *Romeo and Juliet* is of special textual interest because it was almost certainly a pirated edition, that is to say it was published without Shakespeare's permission. It may have been made up from the notes of someone who had seen the play acted, or, more likely, one or more of the actors may have deceived their company and for money communicated to the printer what they could remember of the play. As this meant that there was no author's manuscript for the printer to consult, the text of Q1 is, as might be expected, defective in many ways. It is, for example, seven hundred and fifty lines shorter than the version we know today. Nevertheless, it has some importance in that it has some very interesting stage-directions which seem to be an authentic account of what happened on the stage at the earliest performances, and it has a few readings which are preferable to those found in the Second Quarto (Q2) which was published in 1599. Q2 is very similar to the Folio text and is regarded as the official text published by Shakespeare's company of actors as a reply to the pirated Q1, but, even so, the text is obviously defective in places. The printer was careless and the sources he used seem to have been defective. It can be proved that one of these sources was Q1, and this gives that text sufficient authority to make it worth consulting where Q2 provides a doubtful reading. This Macmillan edition has been based upon Q2 but occasionally the Q1 reading has been preferred.

THE SOURCES

Since Chaucer's time, Italy, which had produced so many great writers, had been a fruitful source of material for English writers. Shakespeare set so many of his plays in Italy that over-imaginative critics have suggested that he must have visited it at some stage of his life, but this by no means follows. There had been several Italian versions of the Romeo and Juliet story in the fifteenth century, and about 1530 the names of the lovers were first used by Luigi da Porto. In 1554 Matteo Bandello made the story better known by including it in a collection of short stories which was widely read and led to a French version in 1559 written by Pierre Boaistuau. This, in its turn, was the source of two English versions. The first was a long poem of 3020 lines written by a young poet called Arthur Brooke which was published with the title *The Tragicall Historye of Romeus and Juliet, written first in Italian by Bandell, and nowe in English by Ar. Br.* in 1562. A year later Brooke was drowned in a shipwreck. The second version was one of a collection of prose stories, many of them translations from Boccaccio and Bandello, which William Painter published with the title *Palace of Pleasure* in 1566–7. In writing *Romeo and Juliet*, Shakespeare made little, if any, use of Painter's book, but his debt to Brooke is considerable. Professor Duthie suggests that few editors have appreciated the fullness of the debt, and he says, 'The drama follows the poem not only in incident, but often in word and phrase.' What Shakespeare makes of his sources is, however, always more important than the sources themselves, and with his already sure grasp of dramatic craftsmanship he has transformed Brooke's poem. A great deal can be learned about his craftsmanship and his intentions from a study of these changes. Brooke's text will be found in volume one of *Narrative and Dramatic Sources of Shakespeare*, edited by Geoffrey Bullough. Among the changes it will be found that the pious moral note of Brooke's 'Address to the Reader' with its mention of 'a couple of unfortunate lovers, thralling themselves to unhonest desire . . . abusing the honourable name of lawful marriage' has gone, as has the banishment of the Nurse and the hanging of the poor apothecary. Mercutio and Tybalt are developed out of mere sketches in the poem, and

3

Tybalt's quarrel with Capulet is Shakespeare's invention, as are such incidents as the coming of Paris to the tomb.

But there are more significant changes. The action is enormously speeded up. In the poem the action lasts for the best part of a year and the lovers are secretly married for no less than three months before Romeo's banishment. The play's action is complete in five days, and the feeling of intensity and tragic inevitability, what Coleridge calls 'the precipitation which is the character of the play', is greatly increased by this means. This breathless haste is repeatedly emphasised by Shakespeare's drawing our attention to the time scheme of the play in such phrases as 'Monday . . . Well, Wednesday is too soon' and 'No, not till Thursday'. In spite of this, Shakespeare has come in for some criticism from editors who have seen the action of the play as lasting only four days and have been unable to reconcile this with the Friar's remark that Juliet would continue 'in this borrowed likeness of shrunk death . . . two and forty hours'. As she took the drug on Tuesday night and was found 'dead' on Wednesday morning they have assumed that the final scenes take place on Wednesday night and that 'two and forty hours' must necessarily be wrong. But there is nothing in the text which says she was buried *immediately*, and it could well be that the funeral was on Thursday. Shakespeare's telescoping of Brooke's months into a few days focuses attention on the sheer speed and inevitability of events, but at the same time, as in real life, we are aware of a double time-scheme at work. So much happens in so short a time that we feel that it must have taken longer, and, skilfully, Shakespeare reinforces this effect by references to the past, by the Nurse's talking of the earthquake, by Capulet's talking of his youth, by the allusions to the ancient feud.

As significant a change, and one which takes us to a consideration of Shakespeare's intentions, is the way in which he has deepened the meaning of the play by emphasis on themes such as the relationship of love and hate, of old and young, of order and disorder. It is in such changes that we see his genius at work.

ASSESSMENT

Critical judgement on *Romeo and Juliet* differs widely in estimating its greatness but there is general agreement about its popularity, which, we are told, is second only to that of *Hamlet*. It is not too clear how this popularity rating has been arrived at, but no one would query the play's lasting appeal not only to theatre-goers and readers but to composers, film and television producers. This popularity began early and there is a story that the *Romeo and Juliet* pages in a copy of the First Folio at the Bodleian Library at Oxford University noticeably suffered from the amount of use they experienced at the hands of the under-graduates. At the Restoration in 1660 it was one of the first plays to be revived, and at one time in the eighteenth century it was being performed at both the Covent Garden and Drury Lane theatres. From 1750 to 1800 it was staged every year (with one exception) at Covent Garden. As was usual, during these two centuries there was much interference with the text. In one revised version the lovers lived happily ever after; in another Juliet woke up before the poison had killed Romeo. It was not until 1845 that Shakespeare's text was treated more respectfully but it still had to survive Sir Henry Irving's spectacular produc-tion in the 1880s when the words disappeared among the 'thirteen distinct pictorial scenes' of such an elaborate nature that there could be no hope of the rapid, continuous performance which the 'two hours' traffic' demands. Not that we can afford to feel superior. In recent years we have seen two films of *Romeo and Juliet* in which the words seemed to matter less than the lush scenery and interpolated incident.

In our own time the play's popularity has been very remarkable. What was regarded only ten years ago as a play too 'adult' for schools is now seen as a play which speaks naturally to the young. New standards of frankness and the breaking-down of that kind of Victorian hypocrisy which led Victorian producers to omit Juliet's speech in which she looks forward to the physical delights of marriage – 'Gallop apace, you fiery-footed steeds' – have meant that it is now sufficiently 'respectable' to be a prescribed book. This could, of course, have been the kiss of death, but the play's great virtues, and, among them, its relevance to those problems of life the young are facing, have ensured its continued appeal.

Among the critics it has not been quite so popular. In 1765 Dr Johnson described it as

> one of the most pleasing of our Author's performances. The scenes are busy and various, the incidents numerous and important, the catastrophe irresistibly affecting, and the process of the action carried on with such probability, at least with such congruity, to popular opinions, as tragedy requires.

Later critics have been less generous and more than any other of Shakespeare's plays it has been damned with faint praise. The two main attacks have been that it is not a true tragedy and that it is an immature work, its immaturity showing in an excessive preoccupation with word-play and a failure to integrate satisfactorily all the varied parts of the play. Coleridge was one of the first to voice these criticisms when he wrote in 1811:

> ... in it are to be found specimens, in degree, of all the excellences which he afterwards displayed in his more perfect dramas, but differing from them in being less forcibly evidenced, and less happily combined; all the parts are more or less present, but they are not united with the same harmony.

No one seems to have worried about whether *Romeo and Juliet* was a true tragedy until this century. In F1 it is placed among the tragedies, and it is described as a tragedy on the title pages of Q1 and Q2. A. C. Bradley in *Shakespearean Tragedy* (1904) described it as a 'pure tragedy', but, since then, the charge that it lacked true tragic quality has been pressed home by several critics, who interestingly enough, have used some of Bradley's ideas on the nature of Shakespearean tragedy to support the attack. The essence of the criticism can be seen in these quotations:

> Bad luck as a motive turns to mere chance . . . *Romeo and Juliet* is indeed rich in spells of its own. But as a pattern of the idea of tragedy, it is a failure. (Professor H. B. Charlton)

> *Romeo and Juliet* may fail as a serious tragedy because Shakespeare blurs the focus and never makes up his mind entirely as to who is being punished and for what reason. (Professor D. Stauffer)

There is much that can be questioned here, not least the assumption that there is one acceptable definition of 'tragedy'. The central idea behind this definition is that we are destroyed by what is false within us, that is to say the tragic hero contributes substantially to his own tragic end. This is certainly one acceptable theory but not the only one, and, in spite of it, it remains true that many people seeing *Romeo and Juliet* acted in the theatre have feelings which they would describe as 'tragic'. This may be because Romeo and Juliet are not, in fact, merely victims of circumstance and that there is at least one way in which they can be said to contribute to their own fate. Or it may be that for many of us the appalling sense of waste which is present at the end of the play provides tragic feelings which are quite as intense as those we would have if the hero and heroine were more responsible for their own deaths than they are. Add to this the feeling that it could all so easily have ended differently and that we are left with the tragic and ironic 'If only . . .' on our lips, and we may well ask, 'If this is not tragedy, what is?' We may want to question, too, Professor Stauffer's charge that Shakespeare has not made up his mind entirely as to who is being punished and for what reason. In the last scene the Prince, who acts very much as a chorus figure, significantly says, 'all are punished'. Could it not be argued that this makes the play very serious tragedy indeed? Thomas Hardy once said, 'The best tragedy – highest tragedy – is that of the worthy encompassed by the inevitable'. By using this definition it could be claimed that *Romeo and Juliet* is the best form of tragedy. What emerges from all this is that we must not be awed by critical theories that are untrue to our own experience and are based upon critical criteria which may sound all right in the study but become irrelevant in the theatre.

One wonders to what extent the critics who have dismissed the play as a second-class tragedy have been influenced by their knowledge that it was written by a comparatively young Shakespeare. The second of the continually recurring adverse criticisms – that *Romeo and Juliet* is an immature work – may well owe something to a bias against a writer's more youthful work. Coleridge drew attention to this immaturity in mentioning the lack of harmony, and other critics have mentioned its changes of tone and style. It has been pointed out that whereas some passages are highly decorated, artificial and full of verbal ingenuities, others appear to come more spontaneously from the poet's heart. As one critic puts it, 'at some points Shakespeare is writing as he used to write, at other points he is writing as he is going to write'. We have to consider whether this is a fair criticism or whether Shakespeare might be defended by saying that part of the play's effect depends upon this clash of styles, and that these contrasts are an organic part of it in that they illuminate character and deepen meaning. Lady Capulet's description of Paris, beginning 'Read o'er the volume of young Paris' face', is conventional and artificial and the metaphor becomes tedious, but how much it tells the audience about Lady Capulet! We must remember, too, that Shakespeare's audience loved and admired word-play and that they could relish it not only in comic but in serious situations where double meanings can provide the richness of ambiguity. We must be fair about this. A great deal of the humour we hear on television and radio is still based upon word-play. For Shakespeare, 'verbal juggling' – as it has been deprecatingly called – was a serious artistic technique, a technique which scintillates throughout our play. Dr Johnson described the quibble, or pun, as the 'fatal Cleopatra for which Shakespeare lost the world', but Coleridge was fairer when, in talking about Shakespeare's conceits, that is his fanciful images and startling comparisons, he said,

> In my mind what have often been censured as Shakespeare's conceits are completely justifiable, as belonging to the state, age, or feeling of the individual. Sometimes, when they cannot be vindicated on these grounds, they may well be excused by the taste of his own and of the preceding age: as for instance, in Romeo's speech,
>
> > Here's much to do with hate, but more with love.
> > Why then, O brawling love, O loving hate,
> > O any thing of nothing first created!
> > O heavy lightness, serious vanity,
> > Mis-shapen chaos of well-seeming forms,
> > Feather of lead, bright smoke, cold fire, sick health,
> > Still-waking sleep, that is not what it is!
>
> I dare not pronounce such passages as these to be absolutely unnatural, not merely because I consider the author a much better judge than I can be, but because I can understand and allow for an effort of the mind, when it would describe what it cannot satisfy itself with the description of, to reconcile opposites and qualify contradictions, leaving a middle state of mind more strictly appropriate to the imagination than any other, when it is, as it were, hovering between images.

What Coleridge is saying here is that by means of these opposites Shakespeare is able brilliantly to convey the conflicting emotions felt by Romeo at this stage of the play. Life is seldom simple and by means of his conceits, his oxymorons and paradoxes, Shakespeare is able to show some of its complexity.

But Coleridge does point the way to another potentially damning criticism, rooted in Shakespeare's immaturity, when he says, 'In this tragedy the poet is not entirely blended with the dramatist – at least not in the degree to be afterwards noticed in *Lear, Hamlet, Othello* or *Macbeth*'. We see this idea developed in a more acute form when a modern critic writes, 'While the play is in certain important respects a dramatic failure, it is a great poetic success'. Can it be long, one wonders, before we are being told that, like *King Lear, Romeo and Juliet* is a great play – but unactable? Here again we have criticism which is divorced from the theatre. No play which is 'in certain important respects a dramatic failure' could have survived so well for so long. No one who has had any experience of the play in the theatre could doubt that it is a dramatic success, whatever else its failings might be. It would be as sensible to describe the play as 'a dramatic success but in many important respects a poetic failure'. Would great actors and actresses have queued up to play the leading parts in a play that was a dramatic failure?

It could be said of these critics that some of them are suffering from an over-intellectual and unbalanced approach, but this may be less damaging than what might be called the over-simple, possibly starry-eyed, approach. The classical example of this is George Meredith's description of the play as 'a love-song in dialogue', and even Coleridge was able to talk of it as 'a spring day; gusty and beautiful in the morn, and closing like an April evening with the song of the nightingale'. Because of the nature of the play it is far too easy to talk of the 'buoyant spirit of youth in every line', as Hazlitt does, when it is possible to quote many lines like those in which Capulet mourns his lost youth:

> I have seen the day
> That I have worn a visor and could tell
> A whispering tale in a fair lady's ear,
> Such as would please. 'Tis gone, 'tis gone, 'tis gone.

in which there is no sign of 'buoyancy'. At a lower level this attitude is seen in the description of the play as a 'tale of young love' or 'this great romantic love-song', a cosy attitude which leads inevitably to the woolliness of seeing Capulet as no more than a 'fussy, bustling, hospitable, foolish old gentleman' and the Nurse as a 'friendly, lovable old lady'. *Romeo and Juliet* is, in fact, a complex and highly wrought play and to be fair to it we must not underestimate it. We must not approach it with any preconceived notions of its immaturity or simplicity, and we must rid our minds of hide-bound ideas of the nature of tragedy and the conventions of language. Above all we must see it as a play to be acted and enjoyed.

It is as a living play that Harley Granville-Barker writes about *Romeo and Juliet* in the Second Series of his *Prefaces to Shakespeare*. Of it he says:

> *Romeo and Juliet* is a living tragedy, and this must be the key to its interpreting. It seems to have been Shakespeare's first unquestionable success, proof positive of his quality and token that he was bringing to the theatre something no one else could bring.

Although he, too, has his reservations and sees it as an immature play, he does at least take it out of the study and put it firmly on the stage. When we read the play it is so easy to theorise about, for example, Lady Montague's death at the end of the play and forget what might be the most likely reason for it – that the actor playing the part in Shakespeare's company had to take on another part at the end of the play. The stage direction 'Enter Will Kemp' which appears in IV. 5 of Q2 is a fascinating insight into the early staging of the play. We know that Kemp was the leading comic of the company, that he was very popular with the audience of that time, and that it is likely, therefore, that the final comic interlude of that scene was written partly in order to provide him with an opportunity of amusing the crowd. In talking about the meaning of the play, which we shall do next, it will be easy to lose sight of the fact that *Romeo and Juliet* is a *play*. Our appreciation will be enhanced if we remember that the play's meaning is not something that can be precisely identified and that on the stage it is a product of the many factors which make up the performance we are seeing. And in *Romeo and Juliet* there is 'God's plenty'. It is a rich and rewarding theatrical experience in which not only is the audience encouraged to think about some of the great universal qualities of life – of love and hate, age and youth, order and disorder, life and death – but it is entertained with some of the world's finest verse, excited by action which includes a public brawl, duelling, a feast, a wedding and five deaths on stage, and delighted by the music, the colour, the splendour, the humour and the pathos of it all.

THE MEANING OF THE PLAY

Romeo and Juliet are famous as lovers the world over, and it is primarily as a play about love that we tend to regard it. All the world, we are told, loves a lover, and the beauty, intensity and sheer romanticism of the feelings experienced by the lovers may well be what lingers most in the mind after we have seen a performance. Theirs is the height of romantic love, and the balcony scene with lines like,

> How silver-sweet sound lovers' tongues by night,
> Like softest music to attending ears ...

remains, justifiably, one of the most famous in the whole of Shakespeare's writing. This is not our language of love but it is how we would like to speak if we had the gift. It is relevant, too, that in Shakespeare's time the parts of the women were played by boys, and just as Enobarbus has to describe Cleopatra's beauty in his famous speech,

> The barge she sat in, like a burnished throne
> Burned on the water ...

so Romeo works on the audience's imagination with his

> It seems she hangs upon the cheek of night
> As a rich jewel in an Ethiop's ear.

This is ideal love and we are made even more aware of its nature by the way in which Shakespeare contrasts it with several other kinds of love so that his audience can examine relationships, and ponder over the significance. Romeo's doting over Rosaline is skilfully introduced to emphasise the difference between love and infatuation. His feelings for Rosaline are self-centred, self-deceiving and inward-looking – essentially negative. He is in love with the idea of being in love, and Shakespeare gently laughs at an affectation many of us have experienced in growing up. By contrast Romeo's love for Juliet, and hers for him, are rooted in regard for each other, and are positive and crea-tive. Juliet's concern for him shines through such lines as

> The orchard walls are high and hard to climb,
> And the place death, considering who thou art,
> If any of my kinsmen find thee here.
> . . . .
> I would not for the world they saw thee here.

The humanising influence of true love is seen in the remark-able development of both the lovers, a development which is manifest if one compares the Juliet of

> But no more deep will I endart mine eye
> Than your consent gives strength to make it fly

with the Juliet of

> Yea, noise? Then I'll be brief. O happy dagger
> This is thy sheath; there rest, and let me die.

– or the Romeo of the egoistic posturings of Act I with the Romeo who can show such sympathy for the apothecary, for Paris, and even for Tybalt in his 'bloody sheet' in Act V.

For yet further contrast there is the love of Paris for Juliet which can see nothing wrong in an arranged marriage forced on a young girl against her will. Implicit in the cruelty of Capulet and in Paris's

> That 'may be' must be, love, on Thursday next

is Shakespeare's condemnation of this kind of insensitivity to others.

In even starker contrast to the ideal love of Romeo and Juliet is the attitude of the servants, Sampson and Gregory, of Mercutio and the Nurse. For them love is something wholly sexual and physical, and between them they provide the play with its heavy load of bawdry. It is no use euphemistically dodging the presence of this in the play and pretending it doesn't exist. It is there for a purpose, and a bowdlerised *Romeo and Juliet* would be lacking an important element. Part of this purpose is, of course, to provide humour. The 'blue' joke was as popular then as it is now, and Shakespeare gives his audience what it wants and, as so often, makes a virtue out of necessity. The effect of the bawdry is complex. For some it provides a laugh, others will admire its wit, while yet others, including possibly Shakespeare himself, will find it ironic that an audience can laugh at the rapist jokes of Sampson and Gregory who look upon women as mere objects to serve their pleasure. Their violent attitude towards love links them with the violence of the feud, and it could be argued that for people like Sampson and Gregory, love has become hate.

Much of the Nurse's bawdry seems to be unwitting but in her constant references to the physical side of marriage we see that hers also is a very limited view of love. If love is no more than falling backwards and having babies, then obviously Paris will do as well for a husband as Romeo.

The contrast between her coarseness and Juliet's delicacy and sensitivity is well brought out in I. 3 where we meet them both for the first time. In a useful article in the *Critical Quarterly* (Vol. 14, No. 2) Barbara Everest has drawn attention to the great depth and subtlety of the Nurse's long speech in that scene. Juliet's unsullied nature is made all the more remarkable in the light of her relationship with the Nurse, and the contrast between them is dramatically very important as each emphasises the other's qualities. The Nurse is not just a source of comedy.

Mercutio, the other main source of comedy, is also the main vehicle for the play's bawdry. His appearances are structured in such a way that at first his ribald jokes are a sharp and earthy contrast with Romeo's airy word-play about Rosaline, and then a contrast with the romantic scenes in which the lovers meet and fall in love. Here it may be that not only are we aware of the clash between a dirty-joke attitude to love and love at its finest, but that Shakespeare is tempering the extreme sweetness of the love scenes with the sharpness of the bawdry. Only a master of stagecraft, confident in his own powers, would have dared to put a scene of bawdry immediately before the balcony scene, and follow it soon after with another. It would be wrong, however, to see the contrast too much in terms of extremes. The love of Romeo and Juliet is not something merely ethereal. It is a rounded, balanced love in which the physical relationship is eagerly looked forward to but is transformed by the power of their love into something of which Mercutio and the Nurse and the servants know nothing.

There is yet another aspect of love occupying Shakespeare's thoughts – the love between parents and children. He explores this by showing us a great deal of the Capulet family, so much, in fact, that the seemingly pleasanter Montagues must play a lesser part in the action. The love of the Capulets for their daughter is so possessive and tyrannical that when they are crossed by her it turns into a cruelty that questions the very nature of their affection.

> An you be mine, I'll give you to my friend;
> An you be not, hang, beg, starve, die in the streets.

These and other lines spoken by Capulet in III. 4 are so vicious that it is difficult to understand how some critics see him as no worse than an irritable old man. Is parental love no more than this? He is deaf to his daughter's pleading, while Lady Capulet, an even more contemptible figure, likewise treats her brutally. Even the Nurse, as she was bound to do because of the way in which Shakespeare has created her, betrays her charge and fails Juliet in her hour of need by recommending her to forget Romeo and commit bigamy. What then of her love?

Juliet is let down by all these older people to whom she turns in her trouble and is left increasingly isolated. Even the 'comfortable' Friar fails her and flees from the tomb when he discovers the failure of his plans. This rejection of the young by the old illustrates yet another theme of the play. There is much emphasis on the youth of some of the characters and the age of others. Nowadays we hear frequently of what is modishly called the 'generation gap', and it might be thought that this was something exclusively of the twentieth century. Human relationships, however, change very little in essentials from century to century, and Shakespeare had certainly pondered over the 'generation gap' of his time. In *Romeo and Juliet* the feud is kept going by old men who should know better, and, as always happens in war, it is the young who pay the cost. Of the six deaths in the play, five are of young people, and at the end of the play the old join hands over the graves of the young in a pathetic act of contrition and reconciliation which comes too late. Juliet's description of the Nurse as 'ancient damnation' could just as easily be applied to her mother and father. Shakespeare's sense of fairness and balance is such that not all the old are bad and all the young good, but there is no doubt that the dominating impression left by the old is one of deviousness, coldness, egoism and hatred, while the young are seen as more vigorous, generous, warm and loving.

Lady Capulet emerges as one of the most unpleasant women created by Shakespeare, worthy to be seen as an early sketch for the wicked sisters, Goneril and Regan, in *King Lear*. Contempt, malice, cruelty are the signs of the hatred which is her driving force and which links her strongly to Tybalt, who lives by the sword and very appropriately dies by it. Tybalt's hatred is the counterpart among the young of Lady Capulet's extreme hatred among the old. We know exactly what kind of man Tybalt is when he first appears on the stage, and with sword drawn says,

> What, drawn and talk of peace? I hate the word
> As I hate hell, all Montagues and thee.
> Have at thee, coward!

Shakespeare makes him the epitome of that hatred which is so powerful a force in the play and which eventually drives the lovers to their deaths. Hatred and love are often found close together, and *Romeo and Juliet* is almost as much a study of hatred as of love. Shakespeare's interest in opposites and contrasts comes out strongly in the clashes between Tybalt and Benvolio and Tybalt and Romeo. One of the most powerful moments of the play comes when the lovers' first meeting and their beautiful expressions of love are interrupted by Tybalt's

> Fetch me my rapier, boy. What dares the slave
> Come hither, covered with an antic face,
> To fleer and scorn at our solemnity?
> Now by the stock and honour of my kin,
> To strike him dead I hold it not a sin.

The language here brilliantly conveys the idea of hatred as a violent and destructive force, a force which we shall see feed upon itself and lead so many to the grave. Shakespeare will take up this theme again in *King Lear*.

It is proper that the Prince should draw the moral at the end because he too has suffered from the hatred of the two Houses, and he too is essential to our understanding of the play. There is a parallel between his three carefully-structured appearances – at the beginning, middle and end – and his part in the play, and the producer should make his entries imposing and memorable. Just as the play depends on him for its strong framework, so the State depends on him for its law and order. A recurring theme in Shakespeare's plays is the necessity for law and order to be enforced by a strong ruler. In the words of Helen Morris,

> The political moral of *Romeo and Juliet* is the same as that of Shakespeare's histories . . . if you have powerful nobles engaged in feuds with each other, the State and its ordinary citizens will suffer. There must be some central authority, recognised and acknowledged by all, or disaster will follow.

The quarrelling of the Capulets and Montagues is a challenge to the peace and smooth-running of the State, and it is the Prince's duty to keep his 'rebellious subjects' in order. At his first appearance he warns them that they will be punished with death if they break the peace again. They do, Romeo is banished, and the Prince, worried perhaps at his own leniency, goes off with the observation that 'Mercy but murders, pardoning those that kill'. It is left to the Prince to end the play and to draw the obvious conclusions as the two enemies are at last united by their sorrow. With a nice sense of fairness he does not exempt himself from blame:

> And I for winking at your discords too
> Have lost a brace of kinsmen; all are punished.

The problems of law and order will always be with society. Shakespeare's handling of the subject gives some insight into how one distinguished mind looked at them in the context of the sixteenth century.

It would be difficult to discuss the meaning of *Romeo and Juliet* without some reference to the part played by fate and chance, by choice and character. This subject has already been glanced at in the discussion of the play's claim to be a tragedy, but it is more important in the larger context of Shakespeare's intentions. There is undoubtedly an emphasis on the part played by fate. The lovers are 'star-crossed', Romeo sees 'Some consequence yet hanging in the stars' and describes himself as 'fortune's fool', while Juliet makes an appeal to the fickleness of fortune. Again and again the lovers have premonitions of trouble, and from the beginning the audience knows that only their deaths can 'bury their parents' strife'. A sense of the inevitability of disaster is present throughout and makes itself felt even in the lighter moments. Dramatically this is immensely powerful as a strong sense of irony adds to the richness of response. One commentator has suggested that we should regard the play as a 'tragedy of bad luck', and it is certainly a fact that luck is not on the lovers' side. It was cruelly bad luck that the Friar's letter to Romeo was delayed. But is it all as simple as that? Life is never simple and what happens to us is the result of a constantly changing mixture of choice and chance, and the choice will depend very largely upon our characters. What part, if any, does Romeo's choice play in his death?

To describe the moral of *Romeo and Juliet* as 'more haste, less speed' would be a naïve over-simplification, but we ought to take seriously the Friar's warnings about the dangers of haste and impulsiveness, qualities which are characteristic of youth and which expose it to destruction. Here once more, in the meetings of Romeo and the Friar, we see the confrontation of youth and age. Shakespeare's Friar is altogether a more serious and thoughtful person than Brooke's 'superstitious frier', and it is significant and typical of Shakespeare's moderation that he removes

the bigotry which led Brooke to make the Catholic religion
to some extent responsible for the tragedy. We should not
under-estimate the Friar's contribution to the play. Romeo's
impulsiveness is there for all to see, and it is emphasised
by the telescoping of the events of many months into a few
days. No sooner does Romeo see Juliet than he must marry
her, no sooner does he hear that she is dead than he must
buy poison and commit suicide. In spite of the Friar's

> Therefore love moderately, long love doth so;
> Too swift arrives as tardy as too slow . . .

the words 'haste' and 'hie' resound through the play as if
to underline the feeling of precipitancy. As we see the
Friar giving advice, as the old so often do, and Romeo
ignoring it, as the young so often do, we become aware of
two continents of experience completely divorced from each
other. We can do no more than feel the sadness of it all.
Who in these circumstances would want to allot blame or
apportion responsibility? It is enough that we have felt
the transience of the world and become more conscious of
our common humanity.

THE CHARACTERS

ESCALUS, Prince of Verona

MERCUTIO, kinsman of the Prince and friend of Romeo

PARIS, a nobleman, kinsman of the Prince, and suitor of
  Juliet

MONTAGUE, head of a Veronese family at enmity with the
  Capulets

LADY MONTAGUE

ROMEO, son of Montague

BENVOLIO, nephew of Montague and friend of Romeo

ABRAM ⎫
BALTHASAR ⎭ servants of Montague

CAPULET, head of a Veronese family at enmity with the
  Montagues

LADY CAPULET

JULIET, daughter of Capulet

TYBALT, nephew of Lady Capulet

An old man of the Capulet family

NURSE to Juliet

PETER, servant to Juliet's Nurse

SAMPSON ⎫
GREGORY ⎭ servants of Capulet

FRIAR LAWRENCE ⎫
FRIAR JOHN ⎭ Franciscan monks

An APOTHECARY of Mantua

A CHORUS

Citizens of Verona, Musicians, Watchmen, Maskers, Torchbearers, Pages, Servants

PROLOGUE

The Prologue is spoken by the Chorus, a single speaker probably wearing a black cloak, who sets the scene, gives a brief outline of the story, and, most important, tells the audience that Romeo and Juliet will die. Shakespeare prefers irony to surprise. Appropriately for a romantic tragedy the Prologue is a sonnet, a fourteen-line poem used by Elizabethan poets for love poems.

[1] both . . dignity *both noble families*

[2] Verona *a town in the northeast of Italy*

[3] mutiny *violence*

[4] Where. . . unclean *Where the bloodshed of civil strife stains the hands of society*

[6] star-crossed *thwarted by the bad influence of the stars – the first of several important references to the part played by fate and the stars. Believers in astrology thought that the stars under which a man was born determined his character and future.*

[7] misadventured *unfortunate*
overthrows *mishaps*

[9] passage *course*
death-marked *foredoomed. A 'mark' was a navigational point for seamen and there is a sense of the lovers' voyage (passage) towards the 'mark' of death*

[12] two . . . traffic *an indication that the play lasted about two hours. There was no curtain at the front of the stage, no interval and no scene-changing in Shakespeare's theatre, and plays were performed more swiftly than they are today.*

[14] What . . . mend *What is omitted here our acting will try to make up for*

PROLOGUE

Enter CHORUS

Two households, both alike in dignity,
  In fair Verona, where we lay our scene,
From ancient grudge break to new mutiny,
  Where civil blood makes civil hands unclean.
From forth the fatal loins of these two foes
A pair of star-crossed lovers take their life;
Whose misadventured piteous overthrows
Doth with their death bury their parents' strife.
The fearful passage of their death-marked love,
  And the continuance of their parents' rage,   10
Which, but their children's end, nought could remove,
  Is now the two hours' traffic of our stage;
The which if you with patient ears attend,
What here shall miss, our toil shall strive to mend.

[*Exit*

25

ACT ONE, scene 1

The feud is first seen through the eyes of the Capulet and Montague servants. Our attention is caught by the bawdy word-play and the ensuing fight. Shakespeare's theatre had no lights to put out or auditorium curtain to pull up. The stage soon fills up with a mass of rioting people, and order is restored only by the arrival of the Prince. It gradually empties and the scene ends as it began, with just two characters on the stage, but whereas the note at the beginning is one of the hard cruelty of lust expressed in coarse sexual punning, the note at the end is of self-indulgent infatuation expressed in conventional romantic verse. Shakespeare has begun his work of contrasting the many different aspects of love.

[1] carry coals   *bear insults*

[2] colliers   *coal sellers*

[3] an . . . draw   *if we're angry we'll draw our swords*

[5] collar   *the hangman's noose. There is much play on words of similar sound.*

[6] moved   *angered – but the word later acquires the meaning 'forced to action' and 'change position'*

[10] stand   *fight*

[13] take the wall   *Rubbish was thrown into the street in Shakespeare's London and the safest place was against the wall. Sampson means that he will force the Montagues into the gutter.*

[16] weakest . . . wall   *the weakest are pushed on one side*

[18] thrust . . . wall   *The punning now becomes sexual. He will assault the Montague maids against the wall.*

[21–2] The quarrel . . men   *The women are not involved in the quarrel*

[27] maidenheads   *i.e. he will rape them*

[28] sense   *a pun on the two meanings of 'sense' – 'meaning' and 'feeling'*

[30] stand   *a bawdy pun*

[31] a pretty . . . flesh   *a virile person*

[32] fish   *a prostitute*

ACT ONE

Scene 1.   *Enter* SAMPSON *and* GREGORY, *Capulet's servants, armed*

SAMPSON Gregory, on my word we'll not carry coals.

GREGORY No, for then we should be colliers.

SAMPSON I mean, an we be in choler, we'll draw.

GREGORY Ay, while you live, draw your neck out of collar.

SAMPSON I strike quickly being moved.

GREGORY But thou art not quickly moved to strike.

SAMPSON A dog of the house of Montague moves me.

GREGORY To move is to stir, and to be valiant is to stand. Therefore if thou art moved, thou runn'st   10 away.

SAMPSON A dog of that house shall move me to stand. I will take the wall of any man or maid of Montague's.

GREGORY That shows thee a weak slave, for the weakest goes to the wall.

SAMPSON 'Tis true, and therefore women being the weaker vessels are ever thrust to the wall. Therefore I will push Montague's men from the wall, and thrust his maids to the wall.   20

GREGORY The quarrel is between our masters and us their men.

SAMPSON 'Tis all one. I will show myself a tyrant. When I have fought with the men, I will be civil with the maids – I will cut off their heads.

GREGORY The heads of the maids?

SAMPSON Ay, the heads of the maids, or their maiden-heads – take it in what sense thou wilt.

GREGORY They must take it in sense that feel it.

SAMPSON Me they shall feel while I am able to stand,   30 and 'tis known I am a pretty piece of flesh.

GREGORY 'Tis well thou art not fish; if thou hadst,

27

[33] poor-john *an inferior kind of fish. Gregory is querying Sampson's boastful virility.*

      tool *sword – but with a sexual pun*

[36] back thee *back you up*

[38] Fear me not *Do not fear that I will run away*
[39] marry *an oath – originally 'By the Virgin Mary'*
[40] take . . . sides *have the law on our side*

[43] list *please*
[44] bite my thumb *an obscene and contemptuous gesture*

[49–50] Is the . . . 'Ay' *While anxious to quarrel they remain basically cowards.*
Enter . . . *Significantly 'Benvolio' means good-intentioned, while 'Tyb' was a common Elizabethan name for a cat.*

[60] Say 'better' *Gregory has seen Tybalt coming and feels braver.*

[65] swashing *slashing*

thou hadst been poor-john. Draw thy tool, here comes two of the house of Montagues.

Enter ABRAHAM *and another* SERVANT

SAMPSON My naked weapon is out. Quarrel, I will back thee.

GREGORY How, turn thy back and run?

SAMPSON Fear me not.

GREGORY No, marry, I fear thee!

SAMPSON Let us take the law of our sides, let them   40
begin.

GREGORY I will frown as I pass by, and let them take it as they list.

SAMPSON Nay, as they dare. I will bite my thumb at them, which is disgrace to them if they bear it.

ABRAHAM Do you bite your thumb at us, sir?

SAMPSON I do bite my thumb, sir.

ABRAHAM Do you bite your thumb at us, sir?

SAMPSON [*Aside to* GREGORY] Is the law of our side if I
say 'Ay'.   50

GREGORY [*Aside to* SAMPSON] No.

SAMPSON No, sir, I do not bite my thumb at you, sir, but I bite my thumb, sir.

GREGORY Do you quarrel, sir?

ABRAHAM Quarrel, sir? No, sir.

SAMPSON But if you do, sir, I am for you. I serve as good a man as you.

ABRAHAM No better.

SAMPSON Well, sir.

Enter BENVOLIO *on one side*, TYBALT *on the other*

GREGORY [*Aside to* SAMPSON] Say 'better'; here comes   60
one of my master's kinsmen.

SAMPSON Yes, better, sir.

ABRAHAM You lie.

SAMPSON Draw if you be men. Gregory, remember thy swashing blow.

They fight

[68] heartless hinds   *a double pun – 'leaderless deer' or 'cowardly servants'*

[71] manage   *use*

[72] hate   *Tybalt's favourite word. We meet hatred and fighting in the play before we meet love.*

[75] bills . . . partisans   *A bill had a blade on a long wooden haft: a partisan was a spear with an axe-head attached.*

[78] A crutch   *A sarcastic reference to Capulet's age. It immediately tells us something about Lady Capulet's character.*

[80] spite   *scornful defiance*

BENVOLIO Part, fools.
> Put up your swords, you know not what you
> do.

TYBALT *comes up*

TYBALT What, are thou drawn among these heartless
> hinds?
> Turn thee Benvolio, look upon thy death.
BENVOLIO I do but keep the peace. Put up thy sword, 70
> Or manage it to part these men with me.
TYBALT What, drawn and talk of peace? I hate the
> word,
> As I hate hell, all Montagues, and thee.
> Have at thee coward!

They fight

Enter three or four CITIZENS *with clubs and partisans*

CITIZENS Clubs, bills, and partisans! Strike, beat
> them down.
> Down with the Capulets! Down with the
> Montagues!

Enter old CAPULET *and* LADY CAPULET

CAPULET What noise is this? Give me my long sword,
> ho!
LADY CAPULET A crutch, a crutch! Why call you for
> a sword?
CAPULET My sword I say! Old Montague is come,
> And flourishes his blade in spite of me.   80

Enter old MONTAGUE *and* LADY MONTAGUE

MONTAGUE Thou villain Capulet! Hold me not, let
> me go.

[82] Thou ... foe *Lady Montague plays a small part but her character is quickly and skilfully drawn.*

[83] Rebellious ... *The Prince, or ruler, was regarded in Shakespeare's time as God's representative on earth and it was his duty to maintain a divinely-created order. The play is structured around his three appearances, and he speaks for the theme, important in all Shakespeare's plays, that it is vital to combat disorder.*

[84] neighbour-stainèd *stained with the blood of neighbours. They have used their swords dishonourably and thus 'profaned' them.*

[86] pernicious *destructive*

[87] purple fountains *streams of blood*

[89] mistempered *both 'forged for an evil purpose' and 'excessively used'*

[90] movèd *angry*

[91] bred ... word *caused by some trivial remark*

[95] grave ... ornaments *sober and appropriate clothes*

[97] Cankered ... peace *Grown rusty through disuse*
cankered *malignant*

[99] Your ... peace *You shall pay with your lives for having broken the peace*

[103] our *the royal plural*
[104] common *public*

[106] set ... new abroach *opened up again this old feud*

LADY MONTAGUE Thou shalt not stir one foot to seek
a foe.

Enter PRINCE ESCALUS, *with his retinue*

PRINCE Rebellious subjects, enemies to peace,
Profaners of this neighbour-stainèd steel –
Will they not hear? – What ho! You men, you
beasts,
That quench the fire of your pernicious rage
With purple fountains issuing from your veins,
On pain of torture, from those bloody hands
Throw your mistempered weapons to the
ground,
And hear the sentence of your movèd Prince.   90
Three civil brawls bred of an airy word,
By thee old Capulet, and Montague,
Have thrice disturbed the quiet of our streets,
And made Verona's ancient citizens
Cast by their grave beseeming ornaments,
To wield old partisans, in hands as old,
Cankered with peace, to part your cankered
hate.
If ever you disturb our streets again,
Your lives shall pay the forfeit of the peace.
For this time all the rest depart away.   100
You Capulet, shall go along with me.
And Montague, come you this afternoon,
To know our further pleasure in this case,
To old Freetown, our common judgement-
place.
Once more, on pain of death, all men depart.
[*Exeunt all but* MONTAGUE, LADY MONTAGUE, *and*
BENVOLIO
MONTAGUE Who set this ancient quarrel new abroach?
Speak nephew, were you by when it began?
BENVOLIO Here were the servants of your adversary,

[111] prepared   *drawn*

[114] hissed   *Benvolio is scornful of Tybalt's boasting.*

[116] on . . . part   *some on one side, some on the other*

[117] parted . . . part   *separated both sides*
[118] Romeo   *Lady Montague's concern for her son is touching and prepares us for his arrival on stage.*

[120] Madam . . .   *Here the style changes to that of the Petrarchan love poetry of Shakespeare's time. Although the audience does not at first realise that it is hearing of Romeo's infatuations, not his love, Shakespeare cleverly suggests the falseness of Romeo's passion by the use of conventional and artificial verse.*
[122] drave   *drove*
[123] sycamore   *a tree associated with forlorn lovers*
[124] rooteth   *grows*
[126] made   *went*
      ware   *aware*
[127] covert   *shelter*
[129] most sought   *most desired to be*
       most   *most people*
[130] Being . . . self   *Benvolio's desire to be alone is such that even his own company is too much for him.*
[131] Pursued . . . his   *Followed my own wish for solitude by not following Romeo who had the same wish. (It was a convention that unhappy lovers liked to be alone.)*
[132] shunned   *avoided*

[138] Aurora   *the Greek mythical goddess of the dawn*

34

And yours, close fighting ere I did approach.
I drew to part them; in the instant came   110
The fiery Tybalt, with his sword prepared,
Which as he breathed defiance to my ears,
He swung about his head and cut the winds,
Who, nothing hurt withal, hissed him in scorn.
While we were interchanging thrusts and
   blows,
Came more and more, and fought on part and
   part,
Till the Prince came, who parted either part.

LADY MONTAGUE O where is Romeo? Saw you him
   today?
Right glad I am he was not at this fray.

BENVOLIO Madam, an hour before the worshipped sun 120
Peered forth the golden window of the east,
A troubled mind drave me to walk abroad,
Where, underneath the grove of sycamore,
That westward rooteth from this city side,
So early walking did I see your son.
Towards him I made; but he was ware of
   me,
And stole into the covert of the wood.
I, measuring his affections by my own,
Which then most sought where most might
   not be found,
Being one too many by my weary self,   130
Pursued my humour, not pursuing his,
And gladly shunned who gladly fled from me.

MONTAGUE Many a morning hath he there been seen,
With tears augmenting the fresh morning's
   dew,
Adding to clouds more clouds with his deep
   sighs,
But all so soon as the all-cheering sun
Should in the farthest east begin to draw
The shady curtains from Aurora's bed,

[139] heavy   *sorrowful*

[142] artificial   *a key word here*

[143] portentous ... prove   *this mood must turn out to be ill-omened*

[147] importuned him   *questioned him persistently*

[149] his ... counsellor   *keeping his feelings to himself*

[151] close   *uncommunicative*

[152] sounding   *being fathomed, measured*

[153] envious   *malicious*

[157] give ... know   *cure his sorrow as learn its cause*
Romeo   *Our first sight of Romeo, like that of Juliet, gives little clue to the rapid development of character which takes place when he really falls in love.*

[158] So please you   *If you please*

[159] grievance ... denied   *cause of sorrow unless he is adamant in his refusal to answer my questions*

[161] true shrift   *a confession of the truth*

[162] Is ... young?   *An ironic opening remark. It is later than Romeo realises.*

[163] new   *recently*

Away from light steals home my heavy son,
And private in his chamber pens himself,   140
Shuts up his windows, locks fair daylight out,
And makes himself an artificial night.
Black and portentous must this humour prove,
Unless good counsel may the cause remove.

BENVOLIO My noble uncle, do you know the cause?

MONTAGUE I neither know it, nor can learn of him.

BENVOLIO Have you importuned him by any means?

MONTAGUE Both by myself and many other friends.
But he, his own affections' counsellor,
Is to himself – I will not say how true –   150
But to himself so secret and so close,
So far from sounding and discovery,
As is the bud bit with an envious worm,
Ere he can spread his sweet leaves to the air,
Or dedicate his beauty to the sun.
Could we but learn from whence his sorrows
     grow,
We would as willingly give cure as know.

Enter ROMEO

BENVOLIO See where he comes. So please you, step
     aside.
I'll know his grievance or be much denied.

MONTAGUE I would thou wert so happy by thy stay,   160
To hear true shift. Come madam, let's away.
          [*Exeunt* MONTAGUE *and* LADY MONTAGUE

BENVOLIO Good morrow, cousin.

ROMEO   Is the day so young?

BENVOLIO But new struck nine.

ROMEO   Ay me, sad hours seem long.
Was that my father that went hence so fast?

BENVOLIO It was. What sadness lengthens Romeo's
     hours?

ROMEO Not having that which, having, makes them
     short.

37

[171] in his view   *in his appearance. Benvolio is thinking of Cupid, the Roman god of love, who is always depicted as a naked boy with blindfolded eyes.*

[172] in proof   *in experience*

[173-4] whose . . . will   *whose eyes are always blindfolded should even so find ways to make us do what he wants*

[177] hate . . . love   *The opposition and yet nearness of love and hate is one of the main themes of the play. Romeo's torrent of oxymorons (a figure of speech by which contradictory terms are combined) emphasises this and is partly a reflection of the torment in Romeo's mind. It is also in its artificiality a guide to the falseness of Romeo's feeling. He is in love with love rather than with Rosaline.*

[181] well-seeming   *apparently beautiful*

[183] Still-   *Always-*

[184] in this   *in return, or in this feud*

[185] coz   *cousin, but the word is used for any close relative*

[187] transgression   *wrong – by adding Benvolio's sorrow to Romeo's, as the next three lines explain*

[193] purged   *purified*

[196] gall   *poison*
          preserving sweet   *a sweetness that keeps alive*

BENVOLIO In love?

ROMEO Out –

BENVOLIO Of love?

ROMEO Out of her favour where I am in love.   170

BENVOLIO Alas that love, so gentle in his view,
    Should be so tyrannous and rough in proof!

ROMEO Alas that love, whose view is muffled still,
    Should without eyes see pathways to his will.
    Where shall we dine? O me, what fray was
      here?
    Yet tell me not, for I have heard it all.
    Here's much to do with hate, but more with
      love.
    Why then, O brawling love, O loving hate,
    O any thing of nothing first created!
    O heavy lightness, serious vanity,   180
    Mis-shapen chaos of well-seeming forms,
    Feather of lead, bright smoke, cold fire, sick
      health,
    Still-waking sleep, that is not what it is!
    This love feel I, that feel no love in this.
    Dost thou not laugh?

BENVOLIO   No coz, I rather weep.

ROMEO Good heart, at what?

BENVOLIO   At thy good heart's oppression.

ROMEO Why, such is love's transgression.
    Griefs of mine own lie heavy in my breast,
    Which thou wilt propagate to have it pressed
    With more of thine. This love that thou hast
      shown   190
    Doth add more grief to too much of mine own.
    Love is a smoke made with the fume of sighs,
    Being purged, a fire sparkling in lovers' eyes,
    Being vexed, a sea nourished with lovers' tears.
    What is it else? A madness most discreet,
    A choking gall, and a preserving sweet.
    Farewell my coz.

[197] Soft   *Wait a moment*

[200] some . . . where   *somewhere else*

[201] in sadness   *seriously. Romeo deliberately misunderstands and in the next line takes it to be 'sorrowfully'.*

[204] Bid . . . will   *Romeo suggests that Benvolio's use of the word 'sadness' is as indiscreet as to suggest that a sick man should make his will.*

[207] aimed so near   *was so near the truth*

[208] mark-man   *marksman*

[210–11] Well . . . arrow   *Romeo carries on the archery imagery. It will not be easy to win the lady as she is not willing to be hit by Cupid's arrow, i.e. fall in love.*

[211] Dian's wit   *the wisdom of the Roman goddess, Diana*

[212] And . . . armed   *and is well protected by the impenetrable armour of chastity*

[213] childish   *because Cupid was a boy*
      uncharmed   *unbewitched*

[214] stay . . . of   *wait and allow herself to be attacked by*
      terms   *expressions*

[216] ope   *open. She will not sell herself.*

[218] That . . . store   *That her beauty will die when she dies because she will have no children to carry it on*

[219] still   *always*

[220] sparing   *holding back of her love*

[222] Cuts . . . posterity   *prevents the future from inheriting the beauty she could have bequeathed to it*

[224] To . . . bliss   *To make herself worthy of happiness in heaven*

[226] live dead   *live as if I were dead. Romeo continues his stream of contradictions.*

[230] Examine . . . beauties   *Look at other beautiful women*

BENVOLIO   Soft, I will go along.
        And if you leave me so, you do me wrong.
ROMEO Tut I have lost myself; I am not here.
        This is not Romeo, he's some other where.   200
BENVOLIO Tell me in sadness, who is that you love?
ROMEO What, shall I groan and tell thee?
BENVOLIO   Groan? Why no.
        But sadly tell me who.
ROMEO Bid a sick man in sadness make his will?
        A word ill urged to one that is so ill.
        In sadness cousin, I do love a woman.
BENVOLIO I aimed so near when I supposed you loved.
ROMEO A right good mark-man. And she's fair I love.
BENVOLIO A right fair mark, fair coz, is soonest hit.
ROMEO Well in that hit you miss. She'll not be hit   210
        With Cupid's arrow. She hath Dian's wit,
        And, in strong proof of chastity well armed,
        From love's weak childish bow she lives un-
            charmed.
        She will not stay the siege of loving terms,
        Nor bide th' encounter of assailing eyes,
        Nor ope her lap to saint-seducing gold.
        O she is rich in beauty, only poor
        That, when she dies, with beauty dies her store.
BENVOLIO Then she hath sworn that she will still live
            chaste?
ROMEO She hath, and in that sparing makes huge waste; 220
        For beauty, starved with her severity,
        Cuts beauty off from all posterity.
        She is too fair, too wise; wisely too fair,
        To merit bliss by making me despair.
        She hath forsworn to love, and in that vow
        Do I live dead that live to tell it now.
BENVOLIO Be rulèd by me, forget to think of her.
ROMEO O teach me how I should forget to think.
BENVOLIO By giving liberty unto thine eyes.
        Examine other beauties.

[231] To ... more   *to make me think even more of her exquisite beauty*

[236] passing   *extremely*

[238] passed   *surpassed*

[240] I'll ... debt   *I'll teach you to forget or else die trying*

ACT ONE, scene 2

The plot is rapidly developed. Romeo and Juliet must meet and Capulet's feast provides the opportunity. Benvolio sees in it a way of distracting Romeo from his 'passion' for Rosaline. Shakespeare's constructive skill is seen in the early introduction of the threat to Romeo and Juliet's happiness which lies in Paris's wish to marry her. Introduced later this would not have been so convincing.

[1] bound   *i.e. to keep the peace*

[3] old   *Shakespeare repeatedly emphasises the age of Capulet and Montague. He is concerned with the differences between old and young.*

[4] reckoning   *reputation*

[5] pity ... long   *The tragic irony is intensified by hints such as this that the feud need not have continued.*

[6] suit   *my request to marry Juliet*

[7] saying o'er   *repeating*

[13] marred   *There was at this time a very high rate of death for both mother and child at child-birth.*

[14] Earth ... she   *All my other children have died*

[15] hopeful   *probably in the sense of continuing his family*

[17] My ... part   *My wishes are subordinate to her agreement. Capulet likes to see himself as a considerate father but is to prove otherwise.*

[18] And   *And if*

[19] according voice   *approval*

[20] old accustomed   *according to an old custom*

ROMEO 'Tis the way 230
To call hers, exquisite, in question more.
These happy masks that kiss fair ladies' brows,
Being black, puts us in mind they hide the fair.
He that is strucken blind cannot forget
The precious treasure of his eyesight lost.
Show me a mistress that is passing fair,
What doth her beauty serve, but as a note
Where I may read who passed that passing fair?
Farewell, thou canst not teach me to forget.
BENVOLIO I'll pay that doctrine, or else die in debt. 240
[Exeunt

Scene 2. *Enter* CAPULET, PARIS *and a* SERVANT

CAPULET But Montague is bound as well as I,
In penalty alike; and 'tis not hard, I think,
For men so old as we to keep the peace.
PARIS Of honourable reckoning are you both,
And pity 'tis you lived at odds so long.
But now my lord, what say you to my suit?
CAPULET But saying o'er what I have said before.
My child is yet a stranger in the world,
She hath not seen the change of fourteen years.
Let two more summers wither in their pride 10
Ere we may think her ripe to be a bride.
PARIS Younger than she are happy mothers made.
CAPULET And too soon marred are those so early
made.
Earth hath swallowed all my hopes but she,
She is the hopeful lady of my earth.
But woo her gentle Paris, get her heart;
My will to her consent is but a part.
And she agreed, within her scope of choice
Lies my consent and fair according voice.
This night I hold an old accustomed feast, 20

[22] store *number*

[24] poor *Capulet enjoys being the host but belittles his own possessions.*

[25] Earth-treading stars *Ladies like stars come down to earth. Caroline Spurgeon in* Shakespeare's Imagery *points out that the dominating image in this play is 'light, every form and manifestation of it'.*

[26] lusty *vigorous*

[27] well-apparelled *well-clothed (because April is the month when the flowers and leaves begin to appear)*

[28] limping *because winter is slow to leave*

[29] female buds *girls about to become women*

[32–3] Which . . . none *These lines are probably corrupt. The general sense seems to be that, in choosing his lady, Paris can take into consideration Capulet's daughter but only as one of many, and, in Capulet's estimation – he is again being falsely modest – one of no account.*

[35] Verona *Shakespeare is constantly reminding his audience of the location.*

Servant *The servant is a clown. He introduces several bawdy jokes, confuses trades and their implements, and being illiterate has to ask Romeo to read the list of invitations.*

[40] yard *a yard measure*
    last *a model of the foot on which shoes are made*

[41] pencil *paint-brush*

[45] In good time *He sees Benvolio and Romeo coming and says that they have come at the right moment.*

[46–51] Tut . . . die *Benvolio returns to his argument that the best way Romeo can forget Rosaline is by falling in love with someone else.*

44

Whereto I have invited many a guest,
Such as I love; and you among the store,
One more, most welcome, makes my number
more.
At my poor house look to behold this night
Earth-treading stars that make dark heaven
light.
Such comfort as do lusty young men feel
When well-apparelled April on the heel
Of limping winter treads, even such delight
Among fresh female buds shall you this night
Inherit at my house. Hear all, all see,   30
And like her most whose merit most shall be;
Which on more view of, many – mine being
one –
May stand in number, though in reckoning
none.
Come go with me.
[*To* SERVANT, *giving a paper*] Go sirrah, trudge
about
Through fair Verona, find those persons out
Whose names are written there, and to them
say,
My house and welcome on their pleasure stay.
[*Exeunt* CAPULET *and* PARIS

SERVANT Find them out whose names are written
here! It is written that the shoemaker should
meddle with his yard, and the tailor with his last,   40
the fisher with his pencil, and the painter with his
nets. But I am sent to find those persons whose
names are here writ, and can never find what names
the writing person hath here writ. I must to the
learned. In good time.

Enter BENVOLIO *and* ROMEO

BENVOLIO Tut man, one fire burns out another's
burning,

[49] cures   *is cured by*

[50] to thy eye   *Love was thought of as being caught through the eye.*

[52] Your . . . leaf   *Romeo rejects Benvolio's advice by suggesting that it is trivial and that there is no cure for love. The plantain leaf was used at this time for various first-aid purposes.*

[55] bound . . .   *Romeo describes the inhuman way in which lunatics were then treated.*

[58] God gi' god-den   *God grant you good even, i.e. any time after noon*

[63] rest you merry   *may God keep you merry. The servant is about to go off, supposing from Romeo's riddling answers that he cannot read.*

[66] County   *Count*

[68] Mercutio   *included in the guests as he is a relative of the Prince even though his friendship is more with the Montagues than the Capulets. Capulet has a shrewd sense of rank.*

[70] Rosaline   *the first mention of Romeo's present love. The actor should indicate that the name has a special significance.*

      One pain is lessened by another's anguish;
      Turn giddy, and be holp by backward turning;
      One desperate grief cures with another's
         languish.
      Take thou some new infection to thy eye,   50
      And the rank poison of the old will die.

ROMEO Your plantain leaf is excellent for that.

BENVOLIO For what I pray thee?

ROMEO   For your broken shin.

BENVOLIO Why Romeo, art thou mad?

ROMEO Not mad, but bound more than a madman is;
      Shut up in prison, kept without my food,
      Whipped and tormented, and – God-den good
         fellow.

SERVANT God gi' god-den. I pray, sir, can you read?

ROMEO Ay, mine own fortune in my misery.

SERVANT Perhaps you have learned it without book.   60
  But I pray can you read anything you see?

ROMEO Ay, if I know the letters and the language.

SERVANT Ye say honestly; rest you merry.

ROMEO Stay fellow, I can read.
    'Signior Martino, and his wife and daughters;
    County Anselme, and his beauteous sisters; the lady
    widow of Vitruvio; Signior Placentio, and his
    lovely nieces; Mercutio, and his brother Valentine;
    mine uncle Capulet, his wife, and daughters; my
    fair niece Rosaline, and Livia; Signior Valentio, and   70
    his cousin Tybalt; Lucio, and the lively Helena.'
      A fair assembly. Whither should they come?

SERVANT Up.

ROMEO Whither?

SERVANT To supper; to our house.

ROMEO Whose house?

SERVANT My master's.

ROMEO Indeed I should have asked you that before.

SERVANT Now I 'll tell you without asking. My master
  is the great rich Capulet; and if you be not of the   80

[81] crush *drink. It is the grapes which are crushed but the crushing is transferred metaphorically to the cup of wine.*

[86] unattainted *unprejudiced*

[88] swan a crow *The swan was a symbol of beauty, the crow of ugliness. Light and darkness are again contrasted.*

[89] devout religion *The conventional romantic code saw love as a religion.*

[91–2] And . . liars *His eyes have often drowned in tears for Rosaline without dying. If they lose faith in her now they will be obvious traitors to their cause and should be burned (as heretics were at that time) as liars.*

[94] match *equal. The exaggerated language emphasises the irony of what happens when Romeo meets Juliet.*

[95–100] Tut . . . best *Benvolio suggests that Romeo's eyes are a pair of scales. At present he sees Rosaline in both eyes so that her beauty cannot be outweighed by any other woman's. If he looks at another woman Rosaline will scant (scarcely) appear beautiful at all.*

[102] in . . . own *in my own lady's (Rosaline's) splendour*

ACT ONE, scene 3

Our first impression of Juliet is as different from our final impression, as it is of Romeo. Juliet is seen here as an apparently undeveloped, submissive girl, desirous only of pleasing her parents. The audience is again reminded of the threat of a marriage to Paris, but it is the Nurse who dominates the scene by her verbosity and coarseness. Love to her is largely something earthy, physical and material.

[2] by my maidenhead *The Nurse is fond of her exclamations, frequently religious but placed, ironically enough, in irreligious contexts. Her opening reference to her virginity – at twelve years old! – is significant.*

[3] lady-bird *She remembers that this is not only a term of endearment but a name for a prostitute, and adds 'God forbid', i.e. let it not be so.*

48

house of Montagues, I pray come and crush a cup
of wine. Rest you merry.

[*Exit*

BENVOLIO At this same ancient feast of Capulet's
    Sups the fair Rosaline whom thou so lov'st,
    With all the admirèd beauties of Verona.
    Go thither, and with unattainted eye,
    Compare her face with some that I shall show,
    And I will make thee think thy swan a crow.
ROMEO When the devout religion of mine eye
    Maintains such falsehood, then turn tears to
     fires,   90
    And these who, often drowned, could never die,
    Transparent heretics, be burnt for liars.
    One fairer than my love? The all-seeing sun
    Ne'er saw her match since first the world
     begun.
BENVOLIO Tut, you saw her fair, none else being by,
    Herself poised with herself in either eye.
    But in that crystal scales let there be weighed
    Your lady's love against some other maid
    That I will show you shining at this feast,
    And she shall scant show well that now seems
     best.   100
ROMEO I'll go along, no such sight to be shown,
    But to rejoice in splendour of mine own.

[*Exeunt*

Scene 3. *Enter* LADY CAPULET *and* NURSE

LADY CAPULET Nurse, where's my daughter? Call
    her forth to me.
NURSE Now by my maidenhead – at twelve year old –
    I bade her come. What lamb! What lady-bird!
    God forbid! Where's this girl? What Juliet!

[9] thou's   *you shall*

[10] pretty age   *attractive age, ready for marriage*

[13] teen   *sorrow*

[15] Lammas-tide   *1 August. Shakespeare makes it clear that it is high summer and that Juliet will be fourteen on 31 July, in just over a fortnight's time.*

        odd days   *a few more days*

[16] Even or odd   *The Nurse misunderstands what Lady Capulet means by 'odd'.*

[18] Susan   *the Nurse's daughter. Probably she died as a baby and it was possible for the Nurse to become Juliet's wet nurse, i.e. to breast-feed her.*

[19] of an age   *the same age*

[22] marry   *by Mary*

[23] the earthquake   *Shakespeare knows how the minds of the middle-aged and elderly work when they reminisce.*

[26] wormwood . . . dug   *Wormwood was a bitter plant which was applied to the nipple to discourage the child from feeding there. It is remarkable that at that time babies seem to have been breast-fed for nearly three years.*

[27] Sitting . . . wall   *Shakespeare knows that as people become older they frequently remember the distant past better than what has just happened.*

[28] Mantua   *a town about twenty miles from Verona*

[29] I . . . brain   *I have an excellent memory*

[30] it   *i.e. the baby Juliet*

[31] fool   *here used as a term of affection*

Enter JULIET

JULIET How now? Who calls?

NURSE   Your mother.

JULIET Madam, I am here. What is your will?

LADY CAPULET This is the matter – Nurse, give leave
      awhile,
      We must talk in secret. Nurse, come back
      again,
      I have remembered me, thou's hear our
      counsel.
      Thou knowest my daughter's of a pretty age.   10

NURSE Faith, I can tell her age unto an hour.

LADY CAPULET She's not fourteen.

NURSE   I'll lay fourteen of my teeth,
      And yet to my teen be it spoken, I have but
      four,
      She's not fourteen. How long is it now
      To Lammas-tide?

LADY CAPULET   A fortnight and odd days.

NURSE Even or odd, of all days in the year,
      Come Lammas Eve at night shall she be
      fourteen.
      Susan and she – God rest all Christian souls –
      Were of an age. Well, Susan is with God,
      She was too good for me. But as I said,   20
      On Lammas Eve at night shall she be fourteen;
      That shall she, marry; I remember it well.
      'Tis since the earthquake now eleven years,
      And she was weaned – I never shall forget it –
      Of all the days of the year, upon that day.
      For I had then laid wormwood to my dug,
      Sitting in the sun under the dove-house wall.
      My lord and you were then at Mantua –
      Nay I do bear a brain – but as I said,
      When it did taste the wormwood on the nipple   30
      Of my dug, and felt it bitter, pretty fool,

[32] tetchy . . . with *fretful and find disagreeable*

[33] 'Shake' . . . dove-house *The shaking of the dove-house warned her to get away from the buildings threatened by the earthquake. Barbara Everest suggests that the dove-house, in its aloofness, mocks the shaking earth.*

    trow *assure you*

[36] high-lone *upright by herself*

    by the rood *by the cross on which Christ died*

[38] broke her brow *cut her head*

[40] 'A *He*

[41] Yea *Yes*

[42] fall backward *to be ready for making love. The Nurse's husband was obviously very well suited to her.*

    wit *understanding*

[43] holidame *holiness or holy relics*

[45] about *true*

[46] an *if*

[48] stinted *stopped*

[52] it brow *its brow*

[53] stone *testicle*

[58] And stint . . . I *Juliet is irritated and embarrassed by the Nurse's repetition of her husband's coarse joke. She picks up the Nurse's 'stinted' and puns on her 'Ay' (pronounced 'I').*

[59] mark . . . grace *make you one of His saved souls*

To see it tetchy and fall out with the dug.
'Shake,' quoth the dove-house; 'twas no need,
    I trow,
To bid me trudge.
And since that time it is eleven years,
For then she could stand high-lone; nay by the
    rood,
She could have run and waddled all about;
For even the day before, she broke her brow,
And then my husband – God be with his soul,
'A was a merry man – took up the child.   40
'Yea,' quoth he, 'dost thou fall upon thy face?
Thou wilt fall backward when thou hast more
    wit,
Wilt thou not Jule?' And by my holidame,
The pretty wretch left crying, and said 'Ay'.
To see now how a jest shall come about!
I warrant, an I should live a thousand years,
I never should forget it. 'Wilt thou not Jule?'
    quoth he,
And, pretty fool, it stinted, and said 'Ay'.

LADY CAPULET Enough of this, I pray thee hold thy
    peace.

NURSE Yes madam, yet I cannot choose but laugh,   50
To think it should leave crying and say 'Ay'.
And yet I warrant it had upon it brow
A bump as big as a young cockerel's stone,
A perilous knock, and it cried bitterly.
'Yea,' quoth my husband, 'fall'st upon thy
    face?
Thou wilt fall backward when thou comest to
    age;
Wilt thou not Jule?' It stinted, and said 'Ay'.

JULIET And stint thou too, I pray thee Nurse, say I.

NURSE Peace, I have done. God mark thee to his
    grace;
Thou wast the prettiest babe that e'er I nursed.   60

[61] And . . . once *If I might some day see you married*

[63] Marry . . . 'marry' *By Mary, that word 'marry'*

[65] dispositions *inclination*

[67–8] An honour . . . teat *The Nurse approves of Juliet's description of marriage as an honour, and implies that Juliet's wisdom has come from her while appearing modestly to suggest otherwise.*

[71] count *reckoning*
[72] much . . . years *at about the same age. This would make Lady Capulet about twenty-eight, considerably younger than her husband, but she may be pretending to be younger than she is.*

[76] a . . . wax *a very model, like a wax image*

[81] Read . . . *Lady Capulet begins an elaborate metaphor in which Paris is compared to a book. Its artificiality is an indication of her lack of any genuine feeling.*
[83] married lineament *harmoniously united feature*
[84] one . . . content *they enhance each other*
[86] in . . . eyes *Explanatory notes were generally written in the margins of books.*
[87] unbound lover *Paris is like an unbound book in that he is not yet bound down by marriage.*
[88] cover *wife*
[89–90] The . . . hide *The fair sea is made fairer by the fair fish it hides. Similarly Juliet (the cover) will make Paris (the book) fairer, and will be proud to do so.*
[91–2] That . . . story *When golden clasps (of a book but with a reference to the wedding ring) enclose fair contents, they partake of the admiration with which the contents are regarded. Similarly Juliet will gain from her marriage to Paris.*

And I might live to see thee married once,
I have my wish.

LADY CAPULET Marry, that 'marry' is the very theme
I came to talk of. Tell me daughter Juliet,
How stands your dispositions to be married?

JULIET It is an honour that I dream not of.

NURSE An honour? Were not I thine only nurse,
I would say thou hadst sucked wisdom from
thy teat.

LADY CAPULET Well, think of marriage now. Younger
than you,
Here in Verona, ladies of esteem,   70
Are made already mothers. By my count,
I was your mother much upon these years
That you are now a maid. Thus then in brief:
The valiant Paris seeks you for his love.

NURSE A man, young lady; lady, such a man
As all the world – why he's a man of wax.

LADY CAPULET Verona's summer hath not such a
flower.

NURSE Nay he's a flower; in faith a very flower.

LADY CAPULET What say you, can you love the
gentleman?
This night you shall behold him at our feast.   80
Read o'er the volume of young Paris' face,
And find delight writ there with beauty's pen;
Examine every married lineament,
And see how one another lends content;
And what obscured in this fair volume lies
Find written in the margent of his eyes.
This precious book of love, this unbound
lover,
To beautify him only lacks a cover.
The fish lives in the sea, and 'tis much pride
For fair without the fair within to hide.   90
That book in many's eyes doth share the glory,
That in gold clasps locks in the golden story.

[95] women . . . men *by becoming pregnant*

[97] if . . . move *if his appearance causes me to like him*

[99] your consent *heavy with irony. When she falls in love it is regardless of her parents' consent.*

[100] Madam . . . *What is the effect of this vigorous prose after the artificiality of Lady Capulet's verse?*

[104] County stays *Count Paris waits for your decision*

ACT ONE, scene 4

Romeo and his friends are on their way to gatecrash Capulet's feast. They will be wearing masks and are in festive mood in spite of Romeo's assumed melancholy. Mercutio is introduced as a foil to Romeo and becomes one of the principal sources of humour.

Mercutio *The Elizabethan mercurial type was thought to be lively, quick-witted and changeable.*

[1-2] shall . . . apology *shall we make this speech of excuse for arriving uninvited or shall we enter without apology?*

[3] The . . . prolixity *Such long-windedness is no longer fashionable*

[4] hoodwinked *blindfolded*

[5] Tartar's . . . bow *The bows of the Tartars were shaped like Cupid's bow.*

    lath *thin wood*

[6] crow-keeper *a scarecrow or boy employed to scare crows*

[7-8] no . . . prompter *no prologue recited without a book and carried so badly that it is a faint repetition of the prompter's words*

[9] measure *judge*

[10] measure . . . measure *perform a dance with them*

So shall you share all that he doth possess,
By having him, making yourself no less.

NURSE No less! Nay, bigger; women grow by men.

LADY CAPULET Speak briefly; can you like of Paris'
love?

JULIET I'll look to like, if looking liking move.
But no more deep will I endart mine eye
Than your consent gives strength to make it fly.

Enter a SERVANT

SERVANT Madam, the guests are come, supper served 100
up, you called, my young lady asked for, the Nurse
cursed in the pantry, and every thing in extremity.
I must hence to wait; I beseech you follow straight.

LADY CAPULET We follow thee. [*Exit* SERVANT] Juliet,
the County stays.

NURSE Go girl, seek happy nights to happy days.

[*Exeunt*

Scene 4. *Enter* ROMEO, BENVOLIO, MERCUTIO *with five
or six other* MASKERS, *and* TORCHBEARERS

ROMEO What, shall this speech be spoke for our
excuse?
Or shall we on without apology?

BENVOLIO The date is out of such prolixity.
We'll have no Cupid hoodwinked with a
scarf,
Bearing a Tartar's painted bow of lath,
Scaring the ladies like a crow-keeper;
Nor no without-book prologue, faintly spoke
After the prompter, for our entrance.
But let them measure us by what they will,
We'll measure them a measure, and be gone. 10

[11] ambling *dancing*
[12] heavy *sad*

[18] a common bound *the ordinary limits*

[21] pitch *the height a falcon soars*
[23] And . . . love *Mercutio takes Romeo's words and gives them a sexual twist as he is to do frequently. His bawdy puns moderate the romanticism of Romeo.*
[28] Prick . . . down *You will get the better of love when you attack him for attacking you. There is an obvious sexual meaning.*
[29] case *mask*
     visage *face*
[30] A . . . visor *Probably 'an ugly mask for an ugly face'.*
[31] quote *observe*
[32] beetle . . . blush *Mercutio refers to his mask which may have large overhanging (beetle) brows and a red face (blush).*
[34] betake . . . legs *begin to dance*
[35] wantons . . . heart *light-hearted merrymakers*
[36] senseless *The rushes (grass-like leaves spread on the floor) are without feeling. Romeo is saying that the dancers are wasting their time.*
[37] For . . . phrase *For I shall follow the advice of the old proverb that the onlooker (candle-holder) sees the best of the game*
[39] The game . . . done *Another proverb – 'When the play is at its best (the gambler is winning) it's time to leave'*
[40] Tut . . . word *The constable's advice is to be as quiet as a mouse.*
[41] Dun *The punning on done/dun is still not done. 'Done' means finished: 'dun' can mean dark coloured and hence low-spirited; 'dun's the mouse' is a way of saying 'be quiet'; 'Dun' was a common name for a horse; and there was an old Christmas game called 'Dun is in the mire' in which a heavy log was lifted and carried off by the players. It is a tribute to his audience that Shakespeare knew that they could follow most or all of this intricate punning.*

ROMEO Give me a torch; I am not for this ambling.
        Being but heavy, I will bear the light.

MERCUTIO Nay gentle Romeo, we must have you
        dance.

ROMEO Not I, believe me; you have dancing shoes
        With nimble soles; I have a soul of lead
        So stakes me to the ground I cannot move.

MERCUTIO You are a lover; borrow Cupid's wings,
        And soar with them above a common bound.

ROMEO I am too sore empiercèd with his shaft
        To soar with his light feathers; and so bound, 20
        I cannot bound a pitch above dull woe.
        Under love's heavy burden do I sink.

MERCUTIO And to sink in it should you burden love;
        Too great oppression for a tender thing.

ROMEO Is love a tender thing? It is too rough,
        Too rude, too boisterous, and it pricks like
        thorn.

MERCUTIO If love be rough with you, be rough with
        love.
        Prick love for pricking, and you beat love
        down.
        Give me a case to put my visage in.
        A visor for a visor. What care I   30
        What curious eye doth quote deformities?
        Here are the beetle brows shall blush for
        me.

BENVOLIO Come knock and enter, and no sooner in,
        But every man betake him to his legs.

ROMEO A torch for me; let wantons light of heart
        Tickle the senseless rushes with their heels.
        For I am proverbed with a grandsire phrase:
        I'll be a candle-holder and look on;
        The game was ne'er so fair, and I am done.

MERCUTIO Tut, dun's the mouse, the constable's own
        word.   40
        If thou art Dun, we'll draw thee from the mire

59

[42] save-your-reverence *begging your pardon. Mercutio apologises mockingly for making fun of Romeo's love.*

[43] we burn daylight *we're wasting the light of our torches by this delay*

[46–7] Take . . . wits *Understand our real meaning rather than the one which comes from too literal an interpretation of our words based upon the five senses (wits)*

[49] 'tis no wit *it is unwise*

[50] tonight *last night*

[51] lie *tell lies. But Romeo gets the better of Mercutio in the next line.*

[53] Queen Mab *There is no earlier known reference so she may be Shakespeare's invention.*

[54] midwife *because she brings to birth the dreams and fantasies of those who sleep*

[57] atomies *tiny creatures*

[60] joiner *carpenter (the squirrel bites his way through wood)*
     grub *maggot (eating away the inside of the nut)*
[61] Time . . . mind *For longer than one can remember*
[62] spinners' *spiders'*
[63] cover *the canopy of the wagon*
[64] traces *reins*
[66] film *gossamer*

[69] Pricked . . . maid *There was a proverbial saying that worms breed on lazy fingers.*

Of this, save-your-reverence, love, wherein
    thou stickest
Up to the ears. Come, we burn daylight, ho!
ROMEO Nay that's not so.
MERCUTIO   I mean sir, in delay
We waste our lights in vain, like lamps by day.
Take our good meaning, for our judgement sits
Five times in that, ere once in our five wits.
ROMEO And we mean well in going to this mask;
But 'tis no wit to go.
MERCUTIO   Why, may one ask?
ROMEO I dreamt a dream tonight.
MERCUTIO   And so did I.   50
ROMEO Well, what was yours?
MERCUTIO   That dreamers often lie.
ROMEO In bed asleep while they do dream things true.
MERCUTIO O then I see Queen Mab hath been with
    you.
She is the fairies' midwife, and she comes
In shape no bigger than an agate stone
On the fore-finger of an alderman,
Drawn with a team of little atomies
Over men's noses as they lie asleep.
Her chariot is an empty hazel-nut,
Made by the joiner squirrel or old grub,   60
Time out o' mind the fairies' coachmakers.
Her wagon-spokes made of long spinners' legs,
The cover of the wings of grasshoppers,
Her traces of the smallest spider web,
Her collars of the moonshine's watery beams,
Her whip of cricket's bone; the lash, of film;
Her wagoner, a small gray-coated gnat,
Not half so big as a round little worm
Pricked from the lazy finger of a maid.
And in this state she gallops night by night   70
Through lovers' brains, and then they dream of
    love;

[72] curtsies   *bowing and scraping (to obtain advancement)*

[78] smelling . . . suit   *finding someone who will reward him for presenting a court-petition*

[79] tithe-pig's   *The Church was paid as a tax (tithe) the tenth of any litter of pigs.*

[80] 'a   *he*

[81] benefice   *church living or appointment*

[84] ambuscadoes   *ambushes*

Spanish blades   *Swords from Toledo in Spain were valued for their high quality.*

[85] healths . . . deep   *very deep drinking*

anon   *at once*

[89] plaits the manes   *knots the hair*

[90] bakes . . . hairs   *cakes together the hair tangled by elves*

[92] hag   *fairy – usually an evil one responsible for nightmares*

[94] carriage   *not merely able to carry themselves well, but also able to bear children and the weight of their lovers*

[96] True . . .   *Mercutio's mood seems to change here and he shows a depth of feeling which makes his coming death even more poignant.*

O'er courtiers' knees, that dream on curtsies
 straight;
O'er lawyers' fingers, who straight dream on
 fees;
O'er ladies' lips, who straight on kisses dream,
Which oft the angry Mab with blisters plagues,
Because their breaths with sweetmeats tainted
 are.
Sometime she gallops o'er a courtier's nose,
And then dreams he of smelling out a suit;
And sometime comes she with a tithe-pig's
 tail,
Tickling a parson's nose as 'a lies asleep,   80
Then dreams he of another benefice.
Sometimes she driveth o'er a soldier's neck,
And then dreams he of cutting foreign throats,
Of breaches, ambuscadoes, Spanish blades,
Of healths five fathom deep; and then anon
Drums in his ear, at which he starts and
 wakes,
And being thus frighted swears a prayer or
 two,
And sleeps again. This is that very Mab
That plaits the manes of horses in the night,
And bakes the elf-locks in foul sluttish hairs, 90
Which once untangled much misfortune
 bodes.
This is the hag, when maids lie on their backs,
That presses them and learns them first to bear,
Making them women of good carriage.
This is she –

ROMEO   Peace, peace, Mercutio, peace.
Thou talk'st of nothing.

MERCUTIO   True, I talk of dreams,
Which are the children of an idle brain,
Begot of nothing but vain fantasy,
Which is as thin of substance as the air,

[100] inconstant *unfaithful – because the wind, rebuffed by the frozen north turns to the warm and moist (dew-dropping) south*

[104] blows . . . ourselves *distracts us from our purpose (going to the feast)*

[106–11] I fear . . . death *There is a sombre note of premonition here.*

[107] yet . . . stars *yet to be revealed – another reference to the astrological importance of the stars*

[108] fearful date *period of fear*

[109] expire the term *end the allotted span*

[110] despisèd . . . breast *despicable life enclosed within me*

[111] vile . . . death *evil penalty of death coming before its time*

[112] he *God (or fate)*

ACT ONE, scene 5

A new scene is usually marked here. On the Elizabethan stage the marching about of the characters would indicate a change of locality and the servingmen with their napkins would show that the feast was about to begin. This is the second of the big scenes – the meeting of the lovers – and Shakespeare has cleverly filled in his background of feud and hate. It is against this sombre, threatening background that the lovers grasp at their happiness.

[2] trencher *wooden plate. The speaker is contemptuous of Pot-pan who may be a hired servant.*

[7] joint-stools *stools made by a carpenter*

[8] court-cupboard *a movable display cabinet*

look . . . plate *take care of the silver table utensils*

Good thou *My good fellow*

[9] marchpane *marzipan*

[14] great chamber *the hall of a large house. The scene must be regarded as changing to the great chamber when Capulet and his friends and guests arrive.*

And more inconstant than the wind who 100
   woos
Even now the frozen bosom of the north,
And being angered puffs away from thence,
Turning his side to the dew-dropping south.
BENVOLIO This wind you talk of blows us from
   ourselves.
Supper is done, and we shall come too late.
ROMEO I fear, too early; for my mind misgives
Some consequence, yet hanging in the stars,
Shall bitterly begin his fearful date
With this night's revels, and expire the term
Of a despisèd life closed in my breast,   110
By some vile forfeit of untimely death.
But he that hath the steerage of my course
Direct my sail. On lusty gentlemen.
BENVOLIO Strike drum.

Scene 5. *They march about the stage, and* SERVINGMEN
come forth with napkins.

FIRST SERVINGMAN Where's Potpan, that he helps not
to take away? He shift a trencher? He scrape a
trencher?
SECOND SERVINGMAN When good manners shall lie all
in one or two men's hands, and they unwashed too,
'tis a foul thing.
FIRST SERVINGMAN Away with the joint-stools, remove
the court-cupboard, look to the plate. Good thou,
save me a piece of marchpane, and as thou lovest
me, let the porter let in Susan Grindstone and   10
Nell. Anthony and Potpan!
THIRD SERVINGMAN Ay boy, ready.
FIRST SERVINGMAN You are looked for, and called for,
asked for, and sought for in the great chamber.
FOURTH SERVINGMAN We cannot be here and there too.

[16] Cheerly   *Cheer up*

[16–17] longer . . . all   *a proverbial expression, originally meaning that the last one to live will take everything, but here it is a vague incitement to cheerfulness*

[19] walk a bout   *have a dance*

[21] makes dainty   *makes excuses*

[22] Am . . . now ?   *Have I got near the truth ?*

[28] A . . . hall   *Clear a space for dancing*

[29] knaves   *boys, i.e. servants*
   turn . . . up   *stack the tables*

[31] unlooked-for sport   *i.e. the arrival of the unexpected guests and the dancing*

[35] By'r Lady   *By the Virgin Mary*

[37] nuptial   *wedding*

[38] Pentecost   *Whit Sunday (the seventh Sunday after Easter)*

Cheerly boys, be brisk awhile, and the longer liver
take all.

Enter CAPULET *and* JULIET *and others of his*
house, meeting the GUESTS *and* MASKERS

CAPULET Welcome gentlemen. Ladies that have their
        toes
      Unplagued with corns will walk a bout with
        you.
      Ah, my mistresses, which of you all   20
      Will now deny to dance? She that makes
        dainty,
      She I'll swear hath corns. Am I come near ye
        now?
      Welcome gentlemen. I have seen the day
      That I have worn a visor and could tell
      A whispering tale in a fair lady's ear,
      Such as would please. 'Tis gone, 'tis gone, 'tis
        gone.
      You are welcome, gentlemen. Come, musicians
        play.
      A hall, a hall; give room, and foot it girls.

Music plays, and they dance

      More light you knaves, and turn the tables up;
      And quench the fire, the room is grown too hot. 30
      Ah sirrah, this unlooked-for sport comes well.
      Nay sit, nay sit, good cousin Capulet,
      For you and I are past our dancing days.
      How long is't now since last yourself and I
      Were in a mask?
SECOND CAPULET   By'r Lady, thirty years.
CAPULET What man, 'tis not so much, 'tis not so much.
      'Tis since the nuptial of Lucentio,
      Come Pentecost as quickly as it will,

[42] a ward   *under the care of a guardian*

[43] What . . . hand   *Shakespeare brilliantly contrasts the old talking about the past with the young falling in love in the present. As Benvolio predicted, Romeo has already forgotten about Rosaline and Shakespeare, shrewdly, does not let us see her.*

[47] Ethiop's   *in Elizabethan times, any black African*

[48] Beauty . . . dear   *Beauty too rich for the uses of this world, too valuable for this earth. There is an ironic foreboding.*

[49] So . . . crows   *An echo of Benvolio's ' I will make thee think thy swan a crow'.*

[50] fellows   *companions*

[53] Forswear   *Deny*

[55] This . . .   *From the old to the young: from love to hate. This is a play of contrasts and they are particularly well contrived in this scene. Note how the hard, clipped consonants of Tybalt's rage contrast with the soft vowels of Romeo's adoration.*

[57] antic face   *grotesque mask*

[58] fleer   *sneer*
     solemnity   *festivity*

[59] stock and honour   *honourable stock*

[66] Content. . . coz   *Calm yourself, noble kinsman*

Some five and twenty years, and then we
        masked.
SECOND CAPULET 'Tis more, 'tis more, his son is elder
        sir;   40
        His son is thirty.
CAPULET   Will you tell me that?
        His son was but a ward two years ago.
ROMEO [*To a* SERVINGMAN] What lady's that which
        doth enrich the hand
        Of yonder knight?
SERVINGMAN   I know not sir.
ROMEO O she doth teach the torches to burn bright.
        It seems she hangs upon the cheek of night
        As a rich jewel in an Ethiop's ear;
        Beauty too rich for use, for earth too dear.
        So shows a snowy dove trooping with crows,
        As yonder lady o'er her fellows shows.   50
        The measure done, I'll watch her place of
        stand,
        And, touching hers, make blessèd my rude
        hand.
        Did my heart love till now? Forswear it sight,
        For I ne'er saw true beauty till this night.
TYBALT This by his voice should be a Montague.
        Fetch me my rapier, boy. What dares the slave
        Come hither, covered with an antic face,
        To fleer and scorn at our solemnity?
        Now by the stock and honour of my kin,
        To strike him dead I hold it not a sin.   60
CAPULET Why how now kinsman, wherefore storm
        you so?
TYBALT Uncle, this is a Montague, our foe;
        A villain that is hither come in spite,
        To scorn at our solemnity this night.
CAPULET Young Romeo is it?
TYBALT   'Tis he, that villain Romeo.
CAPULET Content thee gentle coz, let him alone.

[67] 'A   *He*
      portly   *dignified and well-mannered*

[69] To be . . . youth   *The later tragedy is heightened by Capulet's testimony to the excellence of Romeo's character and the implication that the feud is not insoluble. How does this affect our judgement of the haste and secrecy of Romeo and Juliet's marriage?*
      well-governed   *responsible*

[71] disparagement   *dishonour or injury. The laws of hospitality were sacred.*

[75] ill-beseeming semblance   *unsuitable appearance*

[78] goodman boy   *Tybalt is described as neither a gentleman nor an adult. A 'goodman' was one with a rank below that of gentleman.*
      Go to   *an exclamation of annoyance*

[82] set cock-a-hoop   *start a fight*
      the man   *the man of the house, the big man*

[84] saucy   *insolent*

[85] trick   *behaviour*
      scathe   *injure*
      I know what   *I know what I am doing. The meaning is not clear but Capulet may be threatening Tybalt with some loss of favour.*

[86] contrary   *oppose*

[87] Well . . . hearts!   *Capulet interrupts his outburst against Tybalt with remarks addressed to guests and servants. The handling of the blank verse here is masterly.*
      princox   *insolent young boy. Capulet's temper is in keeping with the way in which he treats his daughter later in the play.*

[90-91] Patience . . . greeting   *Patience forced on me by such obstinate anger makes my body shake at this hostile meeting*

[92-3] this . . . gall   *The irony is all the stronger as this 'intrusion' will lead to Tybalt's own death.*

[94-107] If I . . . take   *Romeo and Juliet at their first meeting share a sonnet as if to illustrate the harmony which immediately exists between them. The conventional view of love as a religion is seen again in the imagery but Romeo's utterance is noticeably less self-centred and there is a genuine and sincere passion in the language.*

[95] holy shrine   *i.e. her hand*
      the gentle sin   *i.e. his kiss which smoothes away the rough touch of his hand*

'A bears him like a portly gentleman;
And to say truth, Verona brags of him
To be a virtuous and well-governed youth.
I would not for the wealth of all this town   70
Here in my house do him disparagement.
Therefore be patient, take no note of him;
It is my will, the which if thou respect,
Show a fair presence and put off these frowns,
An ill-beeseeming semblance for a feast.

TYBALT It fits when such a villain is a guest.
I'll not endure him.

CAPULET   He shall be endured.
What goodman boy, I say he shall. Go to,
Am I the master here or you? Go to.
You'll not endure him? God shall mend my   80
soul!
You'll make a mutiny among my guests?
You will set cock-a-hoop, you'll be the man?

TYBALT Why, uncle, 'tis a shame –
CAPULET   Go to, go to,
You are a saucy boy. Is 't so indeed?
This trick may chance to scathe you, I know
what.
You must contrary me? Marry, 'tis time.
Well said, my hearts! – You are a princox, go;
Be quiet, or – More light, more light! – For
shame!
I'll make you quiet. – What, cheerly my hearts!

TYBALT Patience perforce with wilful choler meeting 90
Makes my flesh tremble in their different
greeting.
I will withdraw, but this intrusion shall,
Now seeming sweet, convert to bitterest gall.
                                          [Exit

ROMEO [To JULIET] If I profane with my unworthiest
hand
This holy shrine, the gentle sin is this,

[99] mannerly *proper*
     this *i.e. touching my hand. There is tension between Juliet's
modesty and her love.*

[101] And . . . kiss *And the touch of palms is a kind of kiss. She
puns on 'palmers', who were pilgrims to the Holy Land who brought
back palm leaves.*

[103] Ay . . . prayer *Romeo is pressing for a kiss but Juliet,
fencing with him, hints that he must pray for it.*

[104] let . . . do *i.e. kiss*

[105] grant thou *grant my prayer for a kiss*

[106] Saints . . . sake *The statues of saints do not move though
they answer prayers*

[107] prayer's effect *i.e. a kiss*

[108] purged *cleaned away*

[110] urged *argued*

[111] by th' book *expertly, as if you had studied the art in a book*

[116] withal *with*

[117] lay hold of her *marry her*

[118] the chinks *plenty of money. The Nurse's coarseness of
vocabulary contrasts with the delicacy of the meeting of the lovers
which we have just witnessed.*

[119] dear account *A grievous reckoning – by falling in love I am
now at the mercy of my enemy*

My lips, two blushing pilgrims, ready stand
To smooth that rough touch with a tender
    kiss.
JULIET Good pilgrim, you do wrong your hand too
    much,
Which mannerly devotion shows in this;
For saints have hands that pilgrims' hands do
    touch,   100
And palm to palm is holy palmers' kiss.
ROMEO Have not saints lips, and holy palmers too?
JULIET Ay pilgrim, lips that they must use in prayer.
ROMEO O then dear saint, let lips do what hands do.
    They pray; grant thou, lest faith turn to
    despair.
JULIET Saints do not move, though grant for prayers'
    sake.
ROMEO Then move not, while my prayer's effect I
    take.

Kisses her

Thus from my lips, by thine, my sin is purged.
JULIET Then have my lips the sin that they have
    took.
ROMEO Sin from my lips? O trespass sweetly urged.   110
    Give me my sin again.
JULIET   You kiss by th' book.
NURSE Madam, your mother craves a word with you.
ROMEO What is her mother?
NURSE   Marry, bachelor,
Her mother is the lady of the house,
And a good lady, and a wise and virtuous.
I nursed her daughter that you talked withal.
I tell you, he that can lay hold of her
Shall have the chinks.
ROMEO   Is she a Capulet?
O dear account, my life is my foe's debt.

[121] the . . . unrest *my worry is the greater because things can only get worse*

[123] foolish . . . towards *a simple meal of light refreshments about to be served*

[124] Is . . . so *his reply to whatever excuse for leaving the maskers have made to him*

[125] honest *honourable*

[127] fay *faith*

waxes *grows*

[129] Come . . . *Juliet is shrewd enough to hide her real interest by first asking about two other men.*

[136] My grave . . . bed *Because she will die if she cannot marry him, and, ironically, although she does not know it, she will die if she does marry him. Death is more than once mentioned as Juliet's lover.*

[140] Too . . . unknown *Seen too soon because I saw him before I knew who he was*

[141] Prodigious *Monstrous – and therefore likely to end in misfortune*

[144] withal *with*

Anon *Coming right away*

BENVOLIO Away, be gone, the sport is at the best. 120
ROMEO Ay, so I fear; the more is my unrest.
CAPULET Nay gentlemen, prepare not to be gone;
　　　We have a trifling foolish banquet towards.

　　　　　　They whisper in his ear

　　　Is it e'en so? Why then I thank you all.
　　　I thank you honest gentlemen; good night.
　　　More torches here! Come on then, let's to bed.
　　　Ah sirrah, by my fay, it waxes late.
　　　I'll to my rest.
　　　　　　　　　　　　　　　[*Exeunt*
JULIET Come hither Nurse. What is yond gentleman?
NURSE The son and heir of old Tiberio. 130
JULIET What's he that now is going out of door?
NURSE Marry, that I think be young Petruchio.
JULIET What's he that follows ther that would not
　　　dance?
　　　　　　　　　　　　　　　[*Exit* ROMEO
NURSE I know not.
JULIET Go ask his name – If he be marrièd,
　　　My grave is like to be my wedding-bed.
NURSE His name is Romeo, and a Montague,
　　　The only son of your great enemy.
JULIET My only love sprung from my only hate!
　　　Too early seen unknown, and known too late! 140
　　　Prodigious birth of love it is to me,
　　　That I must love a loathèd enemy.
NURSE What's this, what's this?
JULIET 　　　　　　A rhyme I learned even now
　　　Of one I danced withal. [*One calls within*
　　　　'Juliet!']
NURSE 　　　　　　　　　　　Anon, anon!
　　　Come let's away, the strangers all are gone.
　　　　　　　　　　　　　　　[*Exeunt*

ACT TWO

Chorus *This speech by the Chorus is often omitted in production because, as Dr Johnson pointed out, it adds nothing to the play.*

[1] old desire *Romeo's infatuation for Rosaline*

[2] young affection *Romeo's love for Juliet*

gapes . . . heir *longs to take his place*

[6] Alike *Both Romeo and Juliet*

[7] foe supposed *the person regarded as his enemy*

complain *make his lover's pleas*

[8] And . . . hooks *And she enjoys the sweets of love stealthily and at a terrible risk*

[10] use *are accustomed*

[14] Temp'ring . . . sweet *Alleviating the terrible hardship they face by the immense joy of their love*

ACT TWO, scene I

Romeo hides at the back of the stage while his friends are present. At the beginning of II. 2 he comes forward and the audience should regard him as being in the Capulets' orchard. The Elizabethan audience would have no difficulty in accepting this as they were not used to the naturalistic theatre of today. Mercutio's bawdiness is not just light relief. As Harley Granville-Barker has pointed out in his Prefaces to Shakespeare, *Mercutio's 'full-blooded sensuality is set very purposefully against Romeo's romantic idealism, and the balance and contrast must not be destroyed.' The ambivalence of Shakespeare's approach is well demonstrated by the juxtaposing of this and the next scene.*

[2] earth *body*

centre *The centre of the body, to which everything was thought to gravitate, is the heart, and his heart is now with Juliet.*

ACT TWO

Enter CHORUS

CHORUS Now old desire doth in his death-bed lie,
    And young affection gapes to be his heir.
That fair for which love groaned for and would
    die,
    With tender Juliet matched, is now not
    fair.
Now Romeo is beloved and loves again,
    Alike bewitchèd by the charm of looks;
But to his foe supposed he must complain,
    And she steals love's sweet bait from fearful
    hooks.
Being held a foe, he may not have access
    To breathe such vows as lovers use to swear;   10
And she as much in love, her means much less
    To meet her new-belovèd any where.
But passion lends them power, time means, to
    meet,
    Temp'ring extremities with extreme sweet.
                                  [Exit

Scene 1. *Enter* ROMEO

ROMEO Can I go forward when my heart is here?
    Turn back, dull earth, and find thy centre out.

Enter BENVOLIO *and* MERCUTIO

BENVOLIO Romeo! My cousin Romeo! Romeo!
MERCUTIO   He is wise,
    And on my life hath stolen him home to bed.
BENVOLIO He ran this way and leapt this orchard wall.
    Call, good Mercutio.

[6] conjure   *use magical incantation to make him appear*

[7] Humours   *Moods. Mercutio is making fun of the procedures of* *magicians who often began a spell with a string of names, and of the* *behaviour of the conventional romantic lover with his ever-changing* *moods.*

[11] gossip   *friend*
    Venus   *the Roman goddess of love*

[12] purblind   *quite blind*

[13] Abraham Cupid   *No firm explanation has been given of this.* *'Abraham men' were beggars and it could be that Mercutio is suggest-* *ing that Cupid has the qualities of a cheat and beggar. But 'Abraham'* *could be a misreading of 'Adam'. There was a famous archer called* *Adam Bell who was supposed to have lived about the time of Robin* *Hood.*

[14] When . . . maid   *A well-known ballad told the story of King* *Cophetua's love for Penelophon, the beggar-maid.*

[16] The . . . dead   *Performing apes were trained to act as if* *they were dead.*

[18] high forehead   *High foreheads were thought beautiful. Por-* *traits of the time show that women shaved off their hair in order to* *heighten their foreheads.*

[20] demesnes   *domains*

[21] in thy likeness   *in your own form. Ghosts were thought to be* *able to take many different forms.*

[23-27] This . . . spite   *Literally these lines mean, 'It would* *anger him if one were to raise a spirit, belonging to some other person,* *in the magic circle of his lover, letting it remain there until she had, by* *her magical powers, satisfied it and caused it to disappear.' But there* *is also a strong sexual metaphor throughout.*

[29] raise up him   *i.e. like a conjured spirit*

[31] consorted . . . night   *to be associated with the damp and* *moody night*

[33] hit the mark   *achieve its aim*

[34] medlar tree   *a fruit tree – but Mercutio is punning on* *'meddle' which was a word for sexual activity*

[38] open-arse   *a country name for the fruit of the medlar tree*
    poperin pear   *a variety of pear named after the town of* *Poperinghe in Belgium*

MERCUTIO   Nay I'll conjure too.
      Romeo! Humours! Madman! Passion! **Lover!**
      Appear thou in the likeness of a sigh,
      Speak but one rhyme, and I am satisfied;
      Cry but 'Ay me', pronounce but 'love' and
          'dove';   10
      Speak to my gossip Venus one fair word,
      One nickname for her purblind son and heir,
      Young Abraham Cupid, he that shot so trim,
      When King Cophetua loved the beggar-maid.
      He heareth not, he stirreth not, he moveth
          not;
      The ape is dead, and I must conjure him.
      I conjure thee by Rosaline's bright eyes,
      By her high forehead, and her scarlet lip,
      By her fine foot, straight leg, and quivering
          thigh,
      And the demesnes that there adjacent lie,   20
      That in thy likeness thou appear to us.
BENVOLIO And if he hear thee, thou wilt anger him.
MERCUTIO This cannot anger him; 'twould anger him
      To raise a spirit in his mistress' circle
      Of some strange nature, letting it there stand
      Till she had laid it and conjured it down;
      That were some spite. My invocation
      Is fair and honest; in his mistress' name,
      I conjure only but to raise up him.
BENVOLIO Come, he hath hid himself among these
          trees   30
      To be consorted with the humorous night.
      Blind is his love, and best befits the dark.
MERCUTIO If love be blind, love cannot hit the mark.
      Now will he sit under a medlar tree,
      And wish his mistress were that kind of fruit
      As maids call medlars, when they laugh alone.
      O Romeo that she were, O that she were
      An open-arse and thou a poperin pear.

[39] truckle-bed   *a bed without legs running on small wheels*
[40] field-bed   *bed outdoors on the ground*

ACT TWO, scene 2

The most famous love scene in all literature is linked to the previous scene of coarse ribaldry by a single transitional line, part of a couplet Romeo shares with Benvolio. The transition is achieved with the same sureness of touch that Shakespeare was to achieve later when he introduced comedy into the most tragic moments of his great tragedies.

[1] He . . . wound   *Romeo means that it is easy enough for Mercutio to laugh about the pains of love when he has never been in love himself.*

[6] her maid   *Virgins were regarded as being the servants of Diana, the goddess of chastity and the moon.*
[8] vestal livery   *chaste uniform (worn by those in Diana's service)*
      sick and green   *a suggestion of sickness, youth and the pallor of moonlight*

[13] discourses   *speaks*

[17] spheres   *By 'stars' Shakespeare probably means planets. It was a belief of his time that the planets moved round the earth in hollow concentric crystal spheres.*

[21] airy region   *the sky*

Romeo good night. I'll to my truckle-bed;
This field-bed is too cold for me to sleep.   40
Come, shall we go?
BENVOLIO   Go then, for 'tis in vain
To seek him here that means not to be found.
                                        [*Exeunt*

Scene 2. ROMEO *comes forward*

ROMEO He jests at scars that never felt a wound.

          JULIET *appears at the window*

But soft, what light through yonder window
     breaks?
It is the east and Juliet is the sun.
Arise fair sun and kill the envious moon,
Who is already sick and pale with grief
That thou her maid art far more fair than she.
Be not her maid since she is envious.
Her vestal livery is but sick and green,
And none but fools do wear it; cast it off.
It is my lady, O it is my love.   10
O that she knew she were.
She speaks, yet she says nothing. What of
     that?
Her eye discourses; I will answer it.
I am too bold, 'tis not to me she speaks.
Two of the fairest stars in all the heaven,
Having some business, do entreat her eyes
To twinkle in their spheres till they return.
What if her eyes were there, they in her head?
The brightness of her cheek would shame those
     stars,
As daylight doth a lamp; her eyes in heaven   20
Would through the airy region stream so
     bright

[31] lazy puffing   *The First Quarto had 'lazy pacing' and an editor later proposed 'lazy passing'. Which do you prefer?*

[33] wherefore . . . Romeo   *why are you a Montague?*

[39] Thou . . . Montague   *You would still be yourself even if you weren't a Montague*

[46] owes   *owns*
[47] doff   *put aside*
[48] for thy name   *in exchange for your name*

[50] new baptized   *One is named at baptism. Romeo will take a new name.*

That birds would sing and think it were not
    night.
See how she leans her cheek upon her hand.
O that I were a glove upon that hand,
That I might touch that cheek.

JULIET   Ay me!
ROMEO   She speaks.
O speak again, bright angel, for thou art
As glorious to this night, being o'er my head,
As is a wingèd messenger of heaven
Unto the white upturnèd, wond'ring eyes
Of mortals that fall back to gaze on him,   30
When he bestrides the lazy puffing clouds,
And sails upon the bosom of the air.

JULIET O Romeo, Romeo, wherefore art thou Romeo?
Deny thy father, and refuse thy name.
Or if thou wilt not, be but sworn my love,
And I'll no longer be a Capulet.

ROMEO [Aside] Shall I hear more, or shall I speak at
    this?

JULIET 'Tis but thy name that is my enemy.
Thou art thy self, though not a Montague.
What's Montague? It is nor hand nor foot,   40
Nor arm nor face, nor any other part
Belonging to a man. O be some other name.
What's in a name? That which we call a rose
By any other name would smell as sweet.
So Romeo would, were he not Romeo called,
Retain that dear perfection which he owes
Without that title. Romeo doff thy name,
And for thy name which is no part of thee,
Take all myself.

ROMEO   I take thee at thy word.
Call me but 'love', and I'll be new baptized.   50
Henceforth I never will be Romeo.

JULIET What man art thou that thus bescreened in
    night

[53] counsel   *private talk*

[53-4] By . . . am   *I do not know how, if I have to use a name, I can tell you who I am.*

[55] dear saint   *These are the words used by Romeo at I. 5. 104.*

[61] dislike   *displease*

[63] The orchard . . . climb   *The rhythm of the line supports the meaning.*

[66] o'erperch   *fly over*

[67-8] For stony . . . attempt   *Romeo is already showing a deeper and more philosophic approach to love.*

[67] stony limits   *walls*

[69] stop   *obstacle*

[70] If . . . thee   *Juliet's concern for Romeo's safety reveals the genuineness of her love for him and reminds us of the dangers lurking in the background.*

[73] am . . . against   *cannot be hurt by*

[76] but   *unless*

[78] proroguèd   *postponed. 'Hate' and 'love' are again juxtaposed in this and the previous line.*

[81] counsel   *advice*

[82] pilot   *The pilot image is echoed at V. 3. 117.*

[83] As that . . . sea   *The sound of the sea can be heard in this line.*

[84] adventure . . . merchandise   *risk everything for such a reward*

So stumblest on my counsel?

ROMEO   By a name
     I know not how to tell thee who I am.
     My name, dear saint, is hateful to myself,
     Because it is an enemy to thee.
     Had I it written, I would tear the word.

JULIET My ears have not yet drunk a hundred words
     Of thy tongue's uttering, yet I know the sound.
     Art thou not Romeo, and a Montague?   60

ROMEO Neither, fair maid, if either thee dislike.

JULIET How cam'st thou hither, tell me, and
     wherefore?
     The orchard walls are high, and hard to climb,
     And the place death, considering who thou art,
     If any of my kinsmen find thee here.

ROMEO With love's light wings did I o'erperch these
     walls,
     For stony limits cannot hold love out,
     And what love can do, that dares love attempt.
     Therefore thy kinsmen are no stop to me.

JULIET If they do see thee, they will murder thee.   70

ROMEO Alack there lies more peril in thine eye
     Than twenty of their swords; look thou but
     sweet,
     And I am proof against their enmity.

JULIET I would not for the world they saw thee here.

ROMEO I have night's cloak to hide me from their eyes,
     And but thou love me, let them find me here.
     My life were better ended by their hate,
     Than death proroguèd, wanting of thy love.

JULIET By whose direction found'st thou out this
     place?

ROMEO By love that first did prompt me to inquire;   80
     He lent me counsel, and I lent him eyes.
     I am no pilot, yet wert thou as far
     As that vast shore washed with the farthest sea,
     I should adventure for such merchandise.

[88] Fain . . . form *Gladly would I be more formal*

[89] farewell compliment *goodbye conventional observance of ceremony*

[92–3] at . . . laughs *a proverbial expression which had its origin in Ovid's Art of Love. Jove (Jupiter), the chief Roman god, was the god of oaths and promises, but lovers' promises were so notoriously unreliable that Jove laughed at them.*

[97] So . . . woo *If you will woo me*
    else *otherwise*

[98] fond *foolishly affectionate*

[99] my . . . light *my behaviour immodest*

[101] more . . . strange *greater skill in seeming to be distant and reserved*

[103] ere . . . ware *before I was aware that you were listening*

[105] And not *And do not*
    light *immodest*

[106] discoverèd *revealed, i.e. darkness has revealed to Romeo her declaration of love*

[109] inconstant *continually changing and therefore unfaithful*

[110] circled orb *the sphere in which the moon moves*

[114] god . . . idolatry *the god I worship. The religious imagery continues very strongly.*

JULIET Thou knowest the mask of night is on my face,
    Else would a maiden blush bepaint my cheek,
    For that which thou hast heard me speak
      tonight.
    Fain would I dwell on form; fain, fain deny
    What I have spoke; but farewell compliment.
    Dost thou love me? I know thou wilt say 'Ay',   90
    And I will take thy word. Yet if thou swear'st,
    Thou mayst prove false; at lovers' perjuries
    They say Jove laughs. O gentle Romeo,
    If thou dost love, pronounce it faithfully.
    Or if thou think'st I am too quickly won,
    I'll frown and be perverse, and say thee nay,
    So thou wilt woo; but else, not for the world.
    In truth, fair Montague, I am too fond,
    And therefore thou mayst think my 'haviour
      light.
    But trust me gentleman, I'll prove more true   100
    Than those that have more cunning to be
      strange.
    I should have been more strange, I must
      confess,
    But that thou overheard'st, ere I was ware,
    My true-love passion. Therefore pardon me,
    And not impute this yielding to light love,
    Which the dark night hath so discoverèd.
ROMEO Lady, by yonder blessèd moon I vow,
    That tips with silver all these fruit-tree tops –
JULIET O swear not by the moon, th'inconstant
      moon,
    That monthly changes in her circled orb,   110
    Lest that thy love prove likewise variable.
ROMEO What shall I swear by?
JULIET   Do not swear at all;
    Or if thou wilt, swear by thy gracious self,
    Which is the god of my idolatry,
    And I'll believe thee.

[116] joy *rejoice*

[117] contract *exchange of vows of love*

[118] rash . . . *Another theme is touched on here – the sheer speed and impulsiveness with which the lovers behave. To what extent, if any, is this a tragedy of precipitancy?*

      unadvised *ill-considered*

[119] lightning *a striking image, repeated at V. 3. 90. T. S. Eliot sees it as significant of the sudden and disastrous power of Juliet's passion.*

[124] that *that heart*

[131] frank *generous*

[133] bounty *capacity for giving. It is hard to recognise the Juliet of I. ii in the speaker of this mature and beautiful testimony to love's infiniteness.*

[141] Too . . . substantial *Too deceitfully sweet to be real*

ROMEO   If my heart's dear love –
JULIET Well, do not swear. Although I joy in thee,
I have no joy of this contract tonight.
It is too rash, too unadvised, too sudden,
Too like the lightning, which doth cease to be
Ere one can say, 'It lightens'. Sweet, good
     night.   120
This bud of love by summer's ripening breath
May prove a beauteous flower when next we
     meet.
Good night, good night. As sweet repose and
     rest
Come to thy heart, as that within my breast.
ROMEO O wilt thou leave me so unsatisfied?
JULIET What satisfaction canst thou have tonight?
ROMEO Th' exchange of thy love's faithful vow for
     mine.
JULIET I gave thee mine before thou didst request it;
And yet I would it were to give again.
ROMEO Wouldst thou withdraw it? For what purpose,
     love?   130
JULIET But to be frank and give it thee again.
And yet I wish but for the thing I have.
My bounty is as boundless as the sea,
My love as deep; the more I give to thee
The more I have, for both are infinite.

NURSE *calls within*

I hear some noise within; dear love adieu.
Anon good nurse! Sweet Montague, be true.
Stay but a little, I will come again.   [*Exit*
ROMEO O blessed, blessed night! I am afeard,
Being in night, all this is but a dream,   140
Too flattering-sweet to be substantial.

Enter JULIET *again*

[143] If . . . *Juliet is refreshingly practical and down to earth, far more so than Romeo. Shakespeare knows his men and women.*
thy . . . love   *the intention of your love*

[145] procure   *arrange*

[146] perform the rite   *go through the wedding ceremony*

[151] By and by   *Immediately*

[153] So . . . soul   *As I hope to be saved from damnation*

[155] to . . . light   *to lack the light of your being here*

[158] falconer's voice   *perhaps a call like the 'Hist' she has just made*

[159] tassel-gentle   *the male peregrine, the noblest of the falcons, trained to respond to the falconer's voice and return to the lure which contained its food*

[160] Bondage is hoarse   *She cannot raise her voice because of the dangers which bind her down.*

[161] Echo   *a Greek goddess of the mountains who wasted away for love of Narcissus until only her voice was left*

JULIET Three words, dear Romeo, and good night
   indeed.
   If that thy bent of love be honourable,
   Thy purpose marriage, send me word to-
    morrow,
   By one that I'll procure to come to thee,
   Where and what time thou wilt perform the
    rite;
   And all my fortunes at thy foot I'll lay,
   And follow thee my lord throughout the world.
NURSE [*Within*] Madam!
JULIET I come, anon – But if thou meanest not well, 150
   I do beseech thee –
NURSE [*Within*] Madam!
JULIET   By and by, I come –
   To cease thy suit, and leave me to my grief.
   Tomorrow will I send.
ROMEO   So thrive my soul –
JULIET A thousand times good night.

            [*Exit*

ROMEO A thousand times the worse, to want thy
   light.
   Love goes toward love as schoolboys from their
    books,
   But love from love, toward school with heavy
    looks.

      Enter JULIET *again*

JULIET Hist, Romeo, hist! O for a falconer's voice
   To lure this tassel-gentle back again.
   Bondage is hoarse, and may not speak aloud, 160
   Else would I tear the cave where Echo lies,
   And make her airy tongue more hoarse than
    mine
   With repetition of 'my Romeo'.
ROMEO It is my soul that calls upon my name.

[167] Romeo . . . *Of this and the following lines Granville-Barker said, 'This is the commonplace made marvellous. What is it, indeed, but the well-worn comic theme of the lovers that cannot say good-bye, turned to pure beauty by the alchemy of the poet?'*

nyas *The First Quarto had 'Madame', the Second Quarto 'Neece', the Second Folio 'Sweete'. It was not until 1955 that J. Dover Wilson, in a brilliant example of textual scholarship, suggested 'nyas', a young hawk which has not left the nest.*

[177] wanton's *spoiled child's*

[179] gyves *shackles*

[188] ghostly father's *spiritual father's (i.e. the priest who looks after his spiritual welfare)*
[189] dear hap *good fortune*

How silver-sweet sound lovers' tongues by
night,
Like softest music to attending ears.

JULIET Romeo!

ROMEO   My nyas.

JULIET   What o'clock tomorrow
Shall I send to thee?

ROMEO   By the hour of nine.

JULIET I will not fail; 'tis twenty year till then.
I have forgot why I did call thee back.   170

ROMEO Let me stand here till thou remember it.

JULIET I shall forget, to have thee still stand there,
Ramemb'ring how I love thy company.

ROMEO And I'll still stay, to have thee still forget,
Forgetting any other home but this.

JULIET 'Tis almost morning; I would have thee
gone,
And yet no farther than a wanton's bird,
That lets it hop a little from her hand,
Like a poor prisoner in his twisted gyves,
And with a silk thread pulls it back again,   180
So loving-jealous of his liberty.

ROMEO I would I were thy bird.

JULIET   Sweet, so would I.
Yet I should kill thee with much cherishing.
Good night, good night. Parting is such sweet
sorrow,
That I shall say 'Good night' till it be morrow.
                                        [*Exit*

ROMEO Sleep dwell upon thine eyes, peace in thy
breast.
Would I were sleep and peace, so sweet to rest.
Hence will I to my ghostly father's cell,
His help to crave, and my dear hap to tell.
                                        [*Exit*

93

ACT TWO, scene 3

A new character appears, Friar Lawrence, who is to play a large part in the tragic development of the story. We see him outside his cell picking flowers and herbs and showing that knowledge of drugs which will be useful later in the story. The series of contrasts continues. The slow, philosophic meditations of the Friar contrast with the instant delights of the previous scene. Helen Morris has pointed out that the Friar is the embodiment of reason as Romeo is that of passion, and that Shakespeare was continually interested in the conflict between 'will' (passion, desire, impulse) and 'reason' (the God-given attribute which helps us to control our desires and impulses). This theme is central in this scene.

[2] Cheq'ring *Making a variegated pattern on*

[3] fleckèd *dappled, spotted*

[4] Titan's wheels *Titan, the Greek sun-god, was imagined as crossing the sky each day in his chariot, the sun.*

[7] osier cage *willow basket*

[8] baleful *poisonous*

[10] What . . . womb *The paradoxes continue. Earth is both the mother from which we come and the grave to which we go.*

[11] divers *different*

[12] We . . . find *The plants (children) are seen as sucking at the bosom of their mother, the earth, which feeds them.*

[14] None . . . some *All have some virtues*

[15] mickle *great*

grace *divine virtue*

[19–20] Nor . . . abuse *Nor nothing so good but perverted from its proper and virtuous use rebels against its true nature and produces evil*

[22] And . . . dignified *And something good may come out of evil. What is the relevance of this to the play?*

Enter Romeo *His entrance here means that he may overhear the next few lines of Friar Lawrence's soliloquy which have a special significance for Romeo.*

[23] infant rind *tender skin*

[24] Poison . . . power *Is found both the power to destroy and to heal*

[25] with . . . part *with its smell cheers each part of the body*

Scene 3. *Enter* FRIAR LAWRENCE

FRIAR LAWRENCE The grey-eyed morn smiles on the
    frowning night,
    Cheq'ring the eastern clouds with streaks of
    light;
    And fleckèd darkness like a drunkard reels
    From forth day's pathway, made by Titan's
    wheels:
    Now ere the sun advance his burning eye,
    The day to cheer, and night's dank dew to dry,
    I must up-fill this osier cage of ours
    With baleful weeds, and precious-juicèd
    flowers.
    The earth that's nature's mother is her tomb;
    What is her burying grave, that is her womb;   10
    And from her womb children of divers kind
    We sucking on her natural bosom find;
    Many for many virtues excellent,
    None but for some, and yet all different.
    O mickle is the powerful grace that lies
    In plants, herbs, stones, and their true
    qualities.
    For nought so vile that on the earth doth live,
    But to the earth some special good doth give,
    Nor aught so good, but strained from that fair
    use,
    Revolts from true birth, stumbling on abuse.   20
    Virtue itself turns vice being misapplied,
    And vice sometime's by action dignified.

Enter ROMEO

    Within the infant rind of this weak flower
    Poison hath residence, and medicine power;
    For this being smelt with that part cheers each
    part;

[26] stays . . . heart *stops the heart and, with it, all the senses*

[27] still *always*

[28] grace . . . will *divine grace and the impulse to give way to one's passions. Is the Friar, unknowingly, moralising on the situation in the play?*

[29] worser *i.e. rude will. This is the Elizabethan double comparative.*

[30] canker *maggot or worm*

[31] Benedicite *God bless you*

[33] argues a distempered *suggests a disturbed*

[35] his watch *awake*

[37] unbruisèd *unhurt (by experience)*
    unstuffed *untroubled*

[40] distemperature *disturbance of the mind*

[41] hit it right *guess it correctly*

[44] Rosaline *What is the purpose of the repeated references to Rosaline?*

[45] ghostly *spiritual*

[46] that . . . woe *the sorrow caused me by that name*

[50] one *i.e. Juliet*
    wounded *i.e. by Cupid's arrows*

[51] both our remedies *we can both be healed*

[52] Within . . . lies *i.e. he can heal them by joining them in holy matrimony.*

[54] intercession *petition*
    steads *benefits*

[55] homely . . . drift *straightforward in your meaning*

[56] Riddling . . . shrift *An ambiguous confession will result in only an unsatisfactory absolution*

Being tasted, stays all senses with the heart.
Two such opposèd kings encamp them still
In man as well as herbs – grace and rude will;
And where the worser is predominant,
Full soon the canker death eats up that plant. 30

ROMEO Good morrow father.

FRIAR LAWRENCE   Benedicite!
What early tongue so sweet saluteth me?
Young son, it argues a distempered head
So soon to bid good morrow to thy bed.
Care keeps his watch in every old man's eye,
And where care lodges, sleep will never lie;
But where unbruisèd youth with unstuffed
      brain
Doth couch his limbs, there golden sleep doth
      reign.
Therefore thy earliness doth me assure
Thou art up-roused by some distemperature; 40
Or if not so, then here I hit it right,
Our Romeo hath not been in bed tonight.

ROMEO That last is true; the sweeter rest was mine.

FRIAR LAWRENCE God pardon sin! Wast thou with
      Rosaline?

ROMEO With Rosaline, my ghostly father? No.
I have forgot that name, and that name's woe.

FRIAR LAWRENCE That's my good son; but where
      hast thou been then?

ROMEO I'll tell thee ere thou ask it me again.
I have been feasting with mine enemy,
Where on a sudden one hath wounded me, 50
That's by me wounded; both our remedies
Within thy help and holy physic lies.
I bear no hatred, blessed man; for lo,
My intercession likewise steads my foe.

FRIAR LAWRENCE Be plain good son, and homely in
      thy drift;
Riddling confession finds but riddling shrift.

[58] rich *an interesting description. Romeo may mean that Capulet is rich in having Juliet as his daughter, but there are other references to Capulet's wealth.*

[60] combined *united*

[63] pass *go along*

[65] Saint Francis *Lawrence is a Franciscan and swears by the saint of his religious order.*

[69] Jesu Maria *By Jesus and Mary*
      brine *salt tears*

[72] To . . . taste! *To give a flavour to a love that now has no flavour*

[79] sentence *wise saying*

[80] Women . . . men *Women may be excused for being unfaithful when men lack the moral strength to be so*

[81] chid'st *rebuked*

ROMEO Then plainly know my heart's dear love is set
On the fair daughter of rich Capulet.
As mine on hers, so hers is set on mine,
And all combined, save what thou must
    combine   60
By holy marriage. When, and where, and how,
We met, we wooed, and made exchange of
    vow,
I'll tell thee as we pass; but this I pray,
That thou consent to marry us today.

FRIAR LAWRENCE Holy Saint Francis, what a change
    is here!
Is Rosaline, that thou didst love so dear,
So soon forsaken? Young men's love then lies
Not truly in their hearts, but in their eyes.
Jesu Maria, what a deal of brine
Hath washed thy sallow cheeks for Rosaline! 70
How much salt water thrown away in waste
To season love, that of it doth not taste!
The sun not yet thy sighs from heaven clears,
Thy old groans yet ring in mine ancient ears;
Lo here upon thy cheek the stain doth sit
Of an old tear that is not washed off yet.
If e'er thou wast thyself, and these woes
    thine,
Thou and these woes were all for Rosaline.
And art thou changed? Pronounce this sen-
    tence then –
Women may fall, when there's no strength in
    men.   80

ROMEO Thou chid'st me oft for loving Rosaline.

FRIAR LAWRENCE For doting not for loving, pupil
    mine.

ROMEO And bad'st me bury love.

FRIAR LAWRENCE   Not in a grave,
To lay one in, another out to have.

ROMEO I pray thee chide me not; her I love now

[86] grace *favour*
     allow *grant*

[87–8] O she ... spell *i.e. Rosaline knew that his expressions of love were recited parrot-fashion without being truly understood.*

[90] In one respect *For one reason*
[91–2] For ... love *The Friar's good intentions are realised, but, ironically, at a terrible price. Does he hope that good (pure love) may come out of evil (the deception he involves himself in)?*
[93] stand *insist*

ACT TWO, scene 4

The action, which can be imagined to take place in a Verona street, advances the play very little. The verbal duelling of the young men is in sharp contrast with the previous two scenes, and there is interest in the meeting of the two chief comic elements – Mercutio and the Nurse.

[2] tonight *last night*
[3] his *i.e. Romeo's*

[6–7] Tybalt ... house *Tybalt's challenge is a reminder of the threatening background against which these young men joke.*

[9] answer it *accept the challenge (invitation to fight). But Mercutio implies in the next line that Romeo is so weak from love of Rosaline that he will be able to answer it only by letter.*

[16] pin *centre. The pin fixed the bull's-eye to the centre of the target.*
[17] cleft *split*
     blind bow-boy's butt-shaft *The butt-shaft was a blunt-headed arrow used for practice. The blind bow-boy is Cupid.*
[20] Cats *Tyb was a common name for a cat.*

Doth grace for grace, and love for love allow.
The other did not so.
FRIAR LAWRENCE   O she knew well
Thy love did read by rote, that could not spell.
But come young waverer, come go with me.
In one respect I'll thy assistant be;   90
For this alliance may so happy prove,
To turn your households' rancour to pure
          love.
ROMEO O let us hence, I stand on sudden haste.
FRIAR LAWRENCE Wisely and slow. They stumble that
          run fast.   [*Exeunt*

Scene. 4. *Enter* MERCUTIO *and* BENVOLIO

MERCUTIO Where the devil should this Romeo be?
          Came he not home tonight?
BENVOLIO Not to his father's; I spoke with his man.
MERCUTIO Why, that same pale hard-hearted wench,
          that Rosaline,
Torments him so, that he will sure run mad.
BENVOLIO Tybalt, the kinsman to old Capulet,
Hath sent a letter to his father's house.
MERCUTIO A challenge on my life.
BENVOLIO Romeo will answer it.
MERCUTIO Any man that can write may answer a   10
          letter.
BENVOLIO Nay, he will answer the letter's master, how
          he dares, being dared.
MERCUTIO Alas poor Romeo, he is already dead,
          stabbed with a white wench's black eye, run
          through the ear with a love-song, the very pin
          of his heart cleft with the blind bow-boy's butt-
          shaft; and is he a man to encounter Tybalt?
BENVOLIO Why what is Tybalt?
MERCUTIO More than Prince of Cats. O he's the   20

[21] captain of compliments *master of the formalities of the duel*

[21–2] as . . . prick-song *as precisely as one follows the notes* (*pricks*) *on a sheet of music. Mercutio is satirising the new fashion in duelling which was with rapiers and great formality. 'Time', 'distance' and 'proportion' are all terms used both in fencing and music.*

[23] he . . . rests *he makes short pauses, as in music*

[24–5] butcher . . . button *so mercilessly accurate that he can pierce a button on his adversary's garment*

[25] duellist *Mercutio uses the latest fashionable word.*

[26] very first house *the best school of fencing*

[26–7] of . . . cause *of the causes leading to the formal challenge*

[27] passado *a forward thrust*

punto reverso *a back-handed blow*

[28] hay *the scoring thrust or thrust home*

[30] pox of *plague on*; antic *absurd*; affecting *affected*

[31] fantasticoes *fops*

tuners of accents *people who try to impress by talking in an affected way and using fashionable words*

[31–2] By Jesu . . . *Mercutio imitates the 'tuners of accents'.*

[32] tall *brave*

[35] strange flies *foreign parasites*

[36] 'pardon me's' *people who indulge in an affected politeness*

stand *insist*

[37] form *manners, but with a pun on 'seat'*

sit . . . bench *they cannot stand the old ones*

[40] roe *a pun on the first syllable of Romeo's name, on roe meaning female deer (dear), and with a sexual quibble*

[42] numbers *poetry*

Petrarch (*1304–74*) *was an Italian poet famous for the love poetry he wrote to Laura de Noves, who did not return his love. Shakespeare has been satirising conventional Petrarchan love poetry in the lines he has given to Romeo before he meets Juliet. Ironically Mercutio does not know that Romeo has left that artificiality behind him.*

[42–4] Laura . . . her *By comparison with Rosaline, Laura was a kitchen servant, but her lover was a better poet than Romeo*

[44–6] Dido *Queen of Carthage who loved Aeneas*; Cleopatra *Queen of Egypt, lover of Julius Caesar and Mark Antony*; Helen *the Grecian beauty whose abduction by Paris started the Trojan war*; Hero *a Greek priestess and lover of Leander*; Thisbe *the lover of Pyramus. All these are regarded by Romeo, says Mercutio, as inferior to his Rosaline.*

[44] dowdy *plain person*

[45] gipsy *someone inferior in attraction*

hildings *worthless creatures*

[46] harlots *immoral women*

[46–7] a grey eye . . . purpose *This becertainly had grey eyes (regarded as attractive) but that makes no difference*

[47] Signior . . . bon jour *He mocks at the use of foreign words.*

courageous captain of compliments! He fights as
you sing prick-song, keeps time, distance, and
proportion; he rests his minim rests, one, two,
and the third in your bosom; the very butcher of
a silk button, a duellist, a duellist; a gentleman
of the very first house, of the first and second
cause. Ah the immortal *passado*, the *punto reverso*,
the hay!

BENVOLIO The what?

MERCUTIO The pox of such antic lisping affecting   30
fantasticoes, these new tuners of accents! 'By
Jesu a very good blade – a very tall man – a very
good whore!' Why, is not this a lamentable thing,
grandsire, that we should be thus afflicted with
these strange flies, these fashion-mongers, these
'pardon-me's', who stand so much on the new
form that they cannot sit at ease on the old bench?
O their bones, their bones!

Enter ROMEO

BENVOLIO Here comes Romeo, here comes Romeo.

MERCUTIO Without his roe, like a dried herring. O   40
flesh, flesh, how art thou fishified! Now is he for
the numbers that Petrarch flowed in. Laura to his
lady was a kitchen-wench – marry, she had a
better love to be-rhyme her – Dido a dowdy,
Cleopatra a gipsy, Helen and Hero hildings and
harlots, Thisbe a grey eye or so, but not to the
purpose – Signior Romeo, *bon jour*. There's a
French salutation to your French slop. You gave
us the counterfeit fairly last night.

ROMEO Good morrow to you both. What counterfeit   50
did I give you?

MERCUTIO The slip sir, the slip; can you not conceive?

ROMEO Pardon good Mercutio, my business was

[48] to your   *to go with your*

  slop   *loose-fitting trousers. He is still wearing his masquerade clothes.*

[48-9] gave . . . counterfeit   *deceived us*

[52] slip   *with a pun on 'slip' meaning a counterfeit coin*

  conceive   *understand*

[55] great   *important*

[56] strain courtesy   *be less polite than he should*

[58] constrains . . . hams   *forces one to bend in the legs. Mercutio puns on 'courtesy' 'curtsy' and introduces further bawdry.*

[60] kindly   *with the extra meaning of 'exactly'*

[61] courteous   *Romeo is in good spirits and joins in the punning.*

[62] very pink   *highest degree*

[63] Pink   *A flower of the dianthus family*

[65] pump   *indoor shoe decorated (pinked) with small holes*

[68] single sole   *The pump usually had a thin sole.*

[69] solely singular   *unrivalled*

[70-1] O . . . singleness   *A poor (single-soled) joke, remarkable only because it is so poor*

[72-3] Come . . . faint   *Part us (as duellists) good Benvolio, I am overwhelmed by Romeo's wit*

[74-5] Switch . . . match   *Spur your wits on as if you were riding a horse or I'll claim the victory in this contest of words*

[76] wild-goose chase   *a type of cross-country horse-race in which the leader has to be followed by the others*

[77] wild-goose   *fool*

[79-80] Was . . . goose?   *Am I equal with you now in this goose business?*

[82] for the goose   *as the silly fool. But goose also has the meaning prostitute.*

[83] I will . . . jest   *Biting by the ear was a sign of affection but Mercutio is being ironic.*

[84] Nay . . . not   *Spare me (proverbial)*

[85] bitter sweeting   *sour sweet apple*

[87] well served in to   *properly served with. Romeo suggests that his wit goes well with Mercutio's foolishness just as sharp apple-sauce goes well with goose.*

[89] cheverel   *the skin of a young goat which stretches easily. The word itself stretches from (in)ch to el(l).*

[90] ell   *forty-five inches*

[91] I . . . out   *I'll take the joke even further*

great, and in such a case as mine a man may
strain courtesy.

MERCUTIO That's as much as to say, such a case as
yours constrains a man to bow in the hams.

ROMEO Meaning to curtsy.

MERCUTIO Thou hast most kindly hit it.   60

ROMEO A most courteous exposition.

MERCUTIO Nay I am the very pink of courtesy.

ROMEO Pink for flower.

MERCUTIO Right.

ROMEO Why, then is my pump well flowered.

MERCUTIO Sure wit. Follow me this jest now, till
thou hast worn out thy pump, that when the
single sole of it is worn, the jest may remain after
the wearing solely singular.

ROMEO O single-soled jest, solely singular for the   70
singleness.

MERCUTIO Come between us good Benvolio, my wits
faint.

ROMEO Switch and spurs, switch and spurs, or I'll cry
a match.

MERCUTIO Nay, if our wits run the wild-goose chase,
I am done; for thou hast more of the wild-goose
in one of thy wits than I am sure I have in
my whole five. Was I with you there for the
goose?   80

ROMEO Thou wast never with me for anything when
thou wast not there for the goose.

MERCUTIO I will bite thee by the ear for that jest.

ROMEO Nay good goose, bite not.

MERCUTIO Thy wit is a very bitter sweeting, it is a
most sharp sauce.

ROMEO And is it not then well served in to a sweet
goose?

MERCUTIO O here's a wit of cheverel that stretches
from an inch narrow to an ell broad.   90

ROMEO I stretch it out for that word 'broad', which,

[93] broad *Various meanings are possible, the most likely being* 'large' *and* 'indecent'.

[94-5] Why ... love? *Mercutio is delighted with his verbal duel with Romeo.*

[95] Now art thou ... *A pun follows on art (are/skill).* **Art** *(skill) is then seen in contrast with nature, and this leads to natural (a born fool).*

[98] lolling *with his tongue hanging out*

[99] bauble *decorated stick carried by a professional fool. The hidden phallic image – seen again in* 'tale' *– carries on the bawdry which runs strongly through this scene.*

[101-2] against the hair *unwillingly*

[103] large *long, coarse – with a bawdy quibble*

[106] occupy *dwell on – with a bawdy quibble*

[108] gear *This can mean either* 'talk' *or* 'clothes', *and can refer to their word-play or to the Nurse's appearance.*

sail *The Nurse, dressed up, looks like a ship under sail.*

[109] a ... smock *a man and a woman*

[112] My fan, Peter *There is humour in the way the Nurse gives herself airs.*

[116] good-den *good-even, i.e. any time after noon*

[119] dial *clock*

prick *point*

[120] what a man *what kind of man? It seems likely that the Nurse would appreciate Mercutio's bawdry but she appears to be shocked.*

[123] By my troth *Upon my word*

[124] quoth 'a *he said*

added to the goose proves thee far and wide a broad goose.

MERCUTIO Why, is not this better now than groaning for love? Now art thou sociable, now art thou Romeo. Now art thou what thou art, by art as well as by nature, for this drivelling love is like a great natural that runs lolling up and down to hide his bauble in a hole.

BENVOLIO Stop there, stop there. 100

MERCUTIO Thou desirest me to stop in my tale against the hair.

BENVOLIO Thou wouldst else have made thy tale large.

MERCUTIO O thou art deceived; I would have made it short, for I was come to the whole depth of my tale, and meant indeed to occupy the argument no longer.

Enter NURSE *and* PETER

ROMEO Here's goodly gear! A sail, a sail!

MERCUTIO Two, two; a shirt and a smock.

NURSE Peter. 110

PETER Anon.

NURSE My fan, Peter.

MERCUTIO Good Peter, to hide her face, for her fan's the fairer face.

NURSE God ye good-morrow gentlemen.

MERCUTIO God ye good-den fair gentlewoman.

NURSE Is it good-den?

MERCUTIO 'Tis no less, I tell ye, for the bawdy hand of the dial is now upon the prick of noon.

NURSE Out upon you, what a man are you! 120

ROMEO One, gentlewoman, that God hath made for himself to mar.

NURSE By my troth, it is well said 'for himself to mar', quoth 'a! Gentlemen, can any of you tell me where I may find the young Romeo?

[129] fault *want*

[131] took *understood. Mercutio laughs at the Nurse for agreeing with Romeo when she does not understand him.*

[133] confidence *a malapropism for 'conference'*

[135] indite *invite. Mercutio makes a deliberate mistake to mock the Nurse's malapropism.*

[136] bawd *an immoral woman who runs a brothel, a hare*
So ho! *the huntsman's cry on sighting the prey*

[138–9] lenten pie *a pie without meat eaten in Lent, the period of abstinence before Easter*

[140] spent *used up*

[141] An old ... *Mercutio's rhyme is based upon two puns: a hare as an 'animal' and an 'immoral woman', and hoar meaning 'old' and whore meaning an 'immoral woman'.*

[145] too ... score *is not worth paying for*

[150] Farewell ... *part of an old ballad*

[152] saucy *insolent*

[153] ropery *roguery*

[154] A gentleman ... *Romeo excuses Mercutio by explaining that he says a great deal that he really doesn't mean.*

[157–8] take him down *get the better of him*

[159] Jacks *low fellows*

ROMEO I can tell you, but young Romeo will be
older when you have found him, than he was when
you sought him. I am the youngest of that name,
for fault of a worse.

NURSE You say well. 130

MERCUTIO Yea, is the worst well? Very well took, i'
faith, wisely, wisely.

NURSE If you be he sir, I desire some confidence
with you.

BENVOLIO She will indite him to some supper.

MERCUTIO A bawd, a bawd, a bawd! So ho!

ROMEO What hast thou found?

MERCUTIO No hare sir, unless a hare sir in a lenten
pie, that is something stale and hoar ere it be
spent. 140

> [*Sings*] An old hare hoar,
> And an old hare hoar,
> Is very good meat in Lent.
> But a hare that is hoar
> Is too much for a score,
> When it hoars ere it be spent.

MERCUTIO Romeo, will you come to your father's?
We'll to dinner thither.

ROMEO I will follow you.

MERCUTIO Farewell ancient lady, farewell, 150
[*Sings*] 'lady, lady, lady'.

                   [*Exeunt* MERCUTIO *and* BENVOLIO

NURSE I pray you sir, what saucy merchant was
this that was so full of his ropery?

ROMEO A gentleman, Nurse, that loves to hear himself
talk, and will speak more in a minute than he will
stand to in a month.

NURSE And 'a speak any thing against me, I'll take
him down, an 'a were lustier than he is, and
twenty such Jacks; and if I cannot, I'll find those

[160] flirt-gills *loose women*
[161] skain's-mates *cut-throat companions(?)*

[163] use . . . pleasure *The humour lies in the presumably unintended bawdry.*

[167] occasion in *opportunity for*

[169] afore *before*

[173-4] lead . . . paradise *take advantage of her*

[177] deal double *deceive*

[181] protest *The Nurse misunderstands Romeo's meaning. His protest that he has no intention of deceiving Juliet is taken as a profession of love.*

[185] mark *listen to*

[189] shrift *confession*

[191] shrived *absolved*

[193] Go . . . shall *It can be assumed that the Nurse doesn't really hesitate about taking Romeo's money.*

that shall. Scurvy knave, I am none of his flirt-gills, 160
I am none of his skain's-mates. [*To Peter*] And
thou must stand by too, and suffer every knave to
use me at his pleasure?

PETER I saw no man use you at his pleasure. If I
had, my weapon should quickly have been out, I
warrant you; I dare draw as soon as another
man, if I see occasion in a good quarrel, and the
law on my side.

NURSE Now afore God I am so vexed, that every part
about me quivers. Scurvy knave! Pray you sir a 170
word: and as I told you, my young lady bid me
inquire you out. What she bid me say, I will keep
to myself. But first let me tell ye, if ye should lead
her in a fool's paradise, as they say, it were a very
gross kind of behaviour, as they say; for the
gentlewoman is young, and therefore if you should
deal double with her, truly it were an ill thing to be
offered to any gentlewoman, and very weak
dealing.

ROMEO Nurse, commend me to thy lady and mistress. 180
I protest unto thee –

NURSE Good heart, and i' faith, I will tell her as much.
Lord, Lord, she will be a joyful woman.

ROMEO What wilt thou tell her, Nurse? Thou dost
not mark me.

NURSE I will tell her sir, that you do protest, which as
I take it is a gentlemanlike offer.

ROMEO Bid her devise
Some means to come to shrift this afternoon,
And there she shall at Friar Lawrence' cell 190
Be shrived and married. Here is for thy pains.

NURSE No truly sir, not a penny.

ROMEO Go to, I say you shall.

NURSE This afternoon sir? Well, she shall be there.

ROMEO And stay good Nurse behind the abbey wall.
Within this hour my man shall be with thee,

[197] tackled stair   *rope ladder*

[198] top-gallant   *summit. The top-gallant was the highest sail.*

[199] be my convoy   *convey me*

[200] quit . . . pains   *recompense you for your trouble*

[204] secret   *capable of keeping a secret*

[205] Two . . . away?   *A proverbial saying meaning that two can keep a secret, but not three.*

[208] prating   *chattering*

[209–10] fain . . . aboard   *gladly claim her*

[210] as lief   *as soon*

[212] properer   *better looking (but see III. 5. 220)*

[214] clout   *piece of cloth*
versal   *universal*

[215] rosemary   *a flower associated with weddings*
a letter   *the same letter*

[217] Ah mocker . . .   *The Nurse thinks that Romeo is mocking her because 'R' was known as the dog's letter as it sounded like a dog's growl. She may also be confused in her ignorance by the belief that words beginning with the letter 'R' should begin with the sound 'ar'.*

[219] sententious   *sentences (malapropism)*

[224] Before . . . apace   *Go in front of me and be quick about it*

ACT TWO, scene 5

A slow-moving, low-toned scene in which the main interest lies in the clash between the directness and impatient excitement of the young Juliet and the insensitive long-windedness of the old Nurse. The location is usually taken to be Capulet's orchard.

[1] nine   *The Nurse has not hurried herself. It was noon when she met Romeo.*

[3] Perchance   *Perhaps*
that's not so   *that can't be true*

And bring thee cords made like a tackled stair,
Which to the high top-gallant of my joy
Must be my convoy in the secret night.
Farewell, be trusty, and I'll quit thy pains.   200
Farewell, commend me to thy mistress.

NURSE Now God in heaven bless thee. Hark you sir.

ROMEO What sayest thou my dear Nurse?

NURSE Is your man secret? Did you ne'er hear say,
Two may keep counsel, putting one away?

ROMEO I warrant thee my man's as true as steel.

NURSE Well, sir, my mistress is the sweetest lady. Lord,
Lord, when 't was a little prating thing. O there is
a nobleman in town, one Paris, that would fain lay
knife aboard; but she, good soul, had as lief see a   210
toad, a very toad, as see him. I anger her sometimes, and tell her that Paris is the properer
man; but I'll warrant you when I say so, she looks
as pale as any clout in the versal world. Doth not
rosemary and Romeo begin both with a letter?

ROMEO Ay Nurse; what of that? Both with an R.

NURSE Ah mocker, that's the dog-name; R is for the –
no, I know it begins with some other letter. And
she hath the prettiest sententious of it, of you and
rosemary, that it would do you good to hear it.   220

ROMEO Commend me to thy lady.

NURSE Ay, a thousand times. Peter!

PETER Anon.

NURSE Before and apace.

[*Exeunt*

Scene 5. *Enter* JULIET

JULIET The clock struck nine when I did send the
        Nurse;
In half an hour she promised to return.
Perchance she cannot meet him – that's not so –

[4] heralds *messengers*
[4–6] Love's . . . hills *another image of light driving away dark*

[6] louring *gloomy-looking and threatening*
[7] Therefore *That is why*
nimble-pinioned *swift-winged*
draw Love *pull the chariot of Venus*

[9] highmost *highest. (It is midday.)*

[14] bandy *strike or throw (a ball as in tennis)*
[15] And . . . me *And his words would strike her (the Nurse) back to me*
[16] But . . . dead *But many old people act as if they were dead*

[25] give . . . awhile *let me have a moment to recover*
[26] jaunce *prancing up and down*

O she is lame! Love's heralds should be
   thoughts,
Which ten times faster glides than the sun's
   beams,
Driving back shadows over louring hills.
Therefore do nimble-pinioned doves draw
   Love,
And therefore hath the wind-swift Cupid
   wings.
Now is the sun upon the highmost hill
Of this day's journey, and from nine till
   twelve   10
Is three long hours, yet she is not come.
Had she affections and warm youthful blood,
She would be swift in motion as a ball;
My words would bandy her to my sweet love,
And his to me.
But old folks, many feign as they were dead,
Unwieldy, slow, heavy and pale as lead.

Enter NURSE *and* PETER

O God she comes! O honey Nurse, what
   news?
Hast thou met with him? Send thy man away.
NURSE Peter, stay at the gate.   20
                        [Exit PETER
JULIET Now good sweet Nurse – O Lord why look'st
   thou sad?
Though news be sad, yet tell them merrily;
If good, thou sham'st the music of sweet
   news
By playing it to me with so sour a face.
NURSE I am aweary, give me leave awhile.
Fie, how my bones ache, what a jaunce have
   I!
JULIET I would thou hadst my bones, and I thy news.

[33-4] The . . . excuse *It has taken you longer to make that excuse for not telling your news than it would have taken to tell your news*

[36] stay the circumstance *wait for the exact details*

[38] simple *foolish. The Nurse teases Juliet.*

[42] be . . . on *are not worth talking about (but there may be a more suggestive meaning)*

[45] Go . . . God *Phrases indicating that she is changing the subject.*

[51] a' t'other *at the other. Juliet is, presumably, rubbing the Nurse's back.*
[52] Beshrew *Confound*
[53] jauncing *prancing*

[56] honest *honourable*

Nay come I pray thee speak; good, good
Nurse speak.

NURSE Jesu, what haste! Can you not stay awhile?
Do you not see that I am out of breath?   30

JULIET How art thou out of breath, when thou hast
breath
To say to me that thou art out of breath?
The excuse that thou dost make in this delay
Is longer than the tale thou dost excuse.
Is thy news good or bad? Answer to that.
Say either, and I'll stay the circumstance.
Let me be satisfied, is 't good or bad?

NURSE Well, you have made a simple choice, you
know not how to choose a man. Romeo? No, not he.
Though his face be better than any man's, yet his   40
leg excels all men's; and for a hand, and a foot, and
a body, though they be not to be talked on, yet
they are past compare. He is not the flower
of courtesy, but I'll warrant him, as gentle as a
lamb. Go thy ways wench, serve God. What,
have you dined at home?

JULIET No, no. But all this did I know before.
What says he of our marriage, what of that?

NURSE Lord, how my head aches, what a head have I!
It beats as it would fall in twenty pieces.   50
My back a' t'other side, ah my back, my back!
Beshrew your heart for sending me about
To catch my death with jauncing up and
down.

JULIET I' faith I am sorry that thou art not well.
Sweet, sweet, sweet nurse, tell me what says
my love?

NURSE Your love says, like an honest gentleman, and
a courteous, and a kind, and a handsome, and I
warrant a virtuous – Where is your mother?

JULIET Where is my mother? Why she is within.
Where should she be? How oddly thou repliest.   60

[62] God's lady   *i.e. the Virgin Mary*
[63] hot   *impatient*
     Marry . . . trow!   *The Nurse expresses impatience and irritation.*

[66] coil   *trouble, fuss*

[71] wanton   *uncontrolled. Juliet is blushing.*

[72] They . . . scarlet   *Your cheeks will redden*
[73] Hie   *Hasten*
     must   *must go*
[75] bird's   *girl's*

[77] But . . . night   *The Nurse again sees love as essentially physical.*

[79] high fortune   *The scene ends on a note of irony which continues in the opening lines of the next scene.*

ACT TWO, scene 6

The lovers meet in the Friar's cell and for them it is the summit of their happiness. There is contrast between their ecstasy and impulsiveness and the Friar's gravity and caution, and ironic and foreboding remarks prepare us for the catastrophe of the next scene.

[1] So . . . upon   *May the heavens so bless*
[2] after-hours   *the future*
[3] Amen   *May it be so – the conventional end of a prayer*
[4] countervail   *outweigh*
[6] close   *join*
    holy words   *i.e. of the marriage ceremony*
[9–15] These . . . slow   *The Friar is worried by the extravagance of Romeo's language and preaches a little sermon.*

'Your love says like an honest gentleman,
"Where is your mother?"'

NURSE   O God's lady dear,
Are you so hot? Marry come up, I trow!
Is this the poultice for my aching bones?
Henceforward do your messages yourself.

JULIET Here's such a coil. Come, what says Romeo?

NURSE Have you got leave to go to shrift today?

JULIET I have.

NURSE Then hie you hence to Friar Lawrence' cell;
There stays a husband to make you a wife.   70
Now comes the wanton blood up in your
    cheeks,
They'll be in scarlet straight at any news.
Hie you to church. I must another way,
To fetch a ladder by the which your love
Must climb a bird's nest soon when it is dark.
I am the drudge, and toil in your delight,
But you shall bear the burden soon at night.
Go. I'll to dinner. Hie you to the cell!

JULIET Hie to high fortune! Honest Nurse, farewell.
                                            [Exeunt

Scene 6. *Enter* FRIAR LAWRENCE *and* ROMEO

FRIAR LAWRENCE So smile the heavens upon this holy
            act
That after-hours with sorrow chide us not.

ROMEO Amen, amen, but come what sorrow can,
It cannot countervail the exchange of joy
That one short minute gives me in her sight.
Do thou but close our hands with holy words,
Then love-devouring death do what he dare,
It is enough I may but call her mine.

FRIAR LAWRENCE These violent delights have violent
            ends,

[10] like . . . powder   *like the meeting of fire and gunpowder*

[11–13] The sweetest . . . appetite   *We can be sickened by an overdose of sweetness*

[12] his   *its*

[13] confounds   *destroys*

[14] long   *lasting*

[15] Too . . . slow   *Those who proceed too quickly arrive no quicker than those who proceed too slowly*

[16–17] O so . . . flint   *The friar comments on the buoyant, light-footed tread of Juliet.*

[18] bestride the gossamers   *ride on the threads of spiders' webs*

[19] idles   *moves lazily*
     wanton   *playful*

[20] light . . . vanity   *insubstantial are the transitory delights of this world*

[21] ghostly confessor   *spiritual father*

[23] As much . . . much   *If Romeo is to pay the thanks of both himself and the Friar (by a kiss?), then Juliet must give as much to Romeo to redress the balance.*

[24–9] if . . . encounter   *if your joy be as great as mine and if you have a greater skill in proclaiming it, sweeten the air around us with your voice, and let the rich music of your tongue reveal the happiness of mind that each of us receives from the other in this precious meeting*

[30–1] Conceit . . . ornament   *Imagination, richer in itself than words can describe, boasts of the reality not of the outward show*

[32] They . . . worth   *To be able to estimate the extent of your love in words is to be poor (compare II. 2. 133)*

[34] sum up sum   *add up the total*

[36] alone   *by yourselves*

And in their triumph die, like fire and powder,   10
Which, as they kiss, consume. The sweetest
  honey
Is loathsome in his own deliciousness,
And in the taste confounds the appetite.
Therefore love moderately, long love doth so;
Too swift arrives as tardy as too slow.

Enter JULIET

Here comes the lady. O so light a foot
Will ne'er wear out the everlasting flint.
A lover may bestride the gossamers
That idles in the wanton summer air,
And yet not fall; so light is vanity.   20

JULIET Good even to my ghostly confessor.
FRIAR LAWRENCE Romeo shall thank thee, daughter,
          for us both.
JULIET As much to him, else is his thanks too much.
ROMEO Ah, Juliet, if the measure of thy joy
          Be heaped like mine, and that thy skill be more
          To blazon it, then sweeten with thy breath
          This neighbour air, and let rich music's tongue
          Unfold the imagined happiness that both
          Receive in either by this dear encounter.
JULIET Conceit, more rich in matter than in words,   30
          Brags of his substance, not of ornament.
          They are but beggars that can count their
            worth;
          But my true love is grown to such excess
          I cannot sum up sum of half my wealth.
FRIAR LAWRENCE Come, come with me, and we will
          make short work,
          For, by your leaves, you shall not stay alone
          Till Holy Church incorporate two in one.
                                              [*Exeunt*

ACT THREE, scene 1

*The violence of this scene is in sharp contrast to the quietness of
the Friar's cell. Romeo is forced by Mercutio's quarrelsome
pride into a duel which threatens his new-found happiness, and
the tragic nature of the lovers' situation now asserts itself. With
Mercutio's death the comedy is finished. The scene in the
sweltering streets of Verona recalls, through the second appearance of the Prince, the opening scene of the play, but this time
the rioting has fatal results.*

[1–4] I pray . . . stirring *Benvolio tries to restrain Mercutio.*

[2] hot *We are reminded that it is high summer.*

    Capels *Capulets*

    abroad *about in the town*

[4] hot . . . stirring *passions easily get out of hand in such hot
weather*

[5] Thou . . . *Mercutio jokingly accuses Benvolio of being
quarrelsome.*

[6–7] claps . . . sword *puts his sword down hard (and provoca-
tively)*

[8–10] by . . . need *as his second drink begins to take effect,
draws his sword on the tavern servant without any provocation*

[12–13] hot . . . mood *a hot-blooded fellow when you're angry*

[13–14] moved . . . moody *provoked to anger*

[14] moody . . . moved *angry at being provoked*

[15] And . . . to? *And moved to what?*

[16] two *a pun on Benvolio's 'to'*

[22] hazel *with a pun on 'hazel' nuts*

    an eye *with a pun on 'I'*

[24] meat *food*

[25] addle *rotten*

[29] wearing . . . Easter *Easter is a time for wearing new
clothes. The tailor may be advertising his new styles by wearing them
somewhat earlier.*

    doublet *jacket*

[30–1] tying . . . riband *supplying his new shoes with old ribbons
– used then as shoe-laces*

ACT THREE

Scene 1. *Enter* BENVOLIO, MERCUTIO, PAGE *and* SERVANTS

BENVOLIO I pray thee good Mercutio, let's retire.
        The day is hot, the Capels are abroad,
        And if we meet, we shall not 'scape a brawl,
        For now, these hot days, is the mad blood
          stirring.

MERCUTIO Thou art like one of these fellows that,
when he enters the confines of a tavern, claps me
his sword upon the table, and says, 'God send me
no need of thee'; and by the operation of the second
cup, draws him on the drawer, when indeed there is
no need.

BENVOLIO Am I like such a fellow?

MERCUTIO Come, come, thou art as hot a Jack in thy
mood as any in Italy, and as soon moved to be
moody, and as soon moody to be moved.

BENVOLIO And what to?

MERCUTIO Nay and there were two such, we should
have none shortly, for one would kill the other.
Thou? Why, thou wilt quarrel with a man that hath
a hair more, or a hair less in his beard than thou
hast. Thou wilt quarrel with a man for cracking
nuts, having no other reason but because thou hast
hazel eyes. What eye but such an eye would spy out
such a quarrel? Thy head is as full of quarrels as
an egg is full of meat, and yet thy head hath been
beaten as addle as an egg for quarrelling. Thou hast
quarrelled with a man for coughing in the street,
because he hath wakened thy dog that hath lain
asleep in the sun. Didst thou not fall out with a
tailor for wearing his new doublet before Easter?
With another for tying his new shoes with old
riband? And yet thou wilt tutor me from quarrelling.

[31–2] tutor . . . quarrelling *teach me not to quarrel*

[33] And *If*

[34] fee-simple *complete possession (a legal term), i.e. his life would not last that long*

[36] O simple! *What a poor joke! But, ironically, he has not even an hour and a quarter of life left.*

[38] By my heel *Mercutio, contemptuously, has no intention of taking to his heels.*

[40] good den *good afternoon*

[41] And but one *Only one*

[43] apt *ready. A significant echo of 'apt' in line 33.*

[44] occasion *cause*

[45–6] take . . . giving *find a reason without my giving you one*

[47] consortest *associate*

[48] Consort? *Mercutio deliberately misunderstands Tybalt by taking his 'consortest' in the sense of 'playing in musical harmony'. As musicians (minstrels) were regarded as servants Mercutio could affect to consider this insulting and a cause for a challenge.*

[50] discords *notes played out of tune; quarrels*
     fiddlestick *i.e. sword – keeping up the musical image*

[51] Zounds *By Christ's wounds (on the cross)*

[54] reason coldly *talk calmly*

[58] my man *the man I'm looking for*

[59] livery *servants' uniform. Mercutio again deliberately misunderstands Tybalt by taking 'my man' as 'my servant'.*

[60] Marry . . . follower *If you go before him to the duelling place he will certainly follow you. Mercutio is maintaining that this is the only sense in which Romeo may be called a follower.*

BENVOLIO And I were so apt to quarrel as thou art,
any man should buy the fee-simple of my life for
an hour and a quarter.

MERCUTIO The fee-simple? O simple!

Enter TYBALT, *and others*

BENVOLIO By my head, here comes the Capulets.

MERCUTIO By my heel, I care not.

TYBALT Follow me close, for I will speak to them.
Gentlemen, good den; a word with one of you. 40

MERCUTIO And but one word with one of us? Couple
it with something, make it a word and a blow.

TYBALT You shall find me apt enough to that sir, an
you will give me occasion.

MERCUTIO Could you not take some occasion without
giving?

TYBALT Mercutio, thou consortest with Romeo.

MERCUTIO Consort? What, dost thou make us
minstrels? An thou make minstrels of us, look to
hear nothing but discords. Here's my fiddlestick, 50
here's that shall make you dance. Zounds, consort!

BENVOLIO We talk here in the public haunt of men.
Either withdraw into some private place,
And reason coldly of your grievances,
Or else depart; here all eyes gaze on us.

MERCUTIO Men's eyes were made to look, and let them
gaze.
I will not budge for no man's pleasure, I.

Enter ROMEO

TYBALT Well, peace be with you sir, here comes my
man.

MERCUTIO But I'll be hanged sir, if he wear your
livery.
Marry, go before to field, he'll be your
follower; 60

[61] Your worship   *said mockingly. Tybalt can call Romeo 'man'*
only in that he will prove to be a man of honour.

[63] villain   *a low-born rascal. A man of honour was bound to*
challenge after such an insult.

[64] reason   *his marriage to Juliet*

[65–6] Doth . . . greeting   *provides a strong reason for my not*
showing the anger which would be natural at such an insult

[68] Boy   *another insult. Tybalt has himself been called a 'boy'*
by Capulet at I. 5. 78.

[71] devise   *imagine*

[73] tender   *value*

[75–7] O calm . . . walk   *Might the catastrophe have been*
avoided but for Mercutio's wilful intervention?

[76] Alla stoccata   *an Italian fencing term meaning 'at the*
thrust'. Mercutio believes that Tybalt with his new-fashioned fencing
has got the better of Romeo.

[77] rat-catcher   *i.e. cat*
        walk   *withdraw to the duelling place*

[80] nine lives   *A cat is said to have nine lives because of its*
ability to escape death.

[80–2] mean . . . eight   *do as I please with and, depending on*
your subsequent behaviour to me, I'll beat the other eight soundly

[83] pilcher   *scabbard*
        ears   *hilt. Mercutio continues to be contemptuous.*

[85] I . . . you   *I am ready for you.*

[86] Gentle . . . up   *Romeo tries desperately to save the peace.*

[87] passado   *further mockery of Tybalt's fencing terms*

[89] forbear   *stop*

[91] bandying   *exchange of blows, brawling*

Your worship in that sense may call him man.

TYBALT Romeo, the love I bear thee can afford
No better term than this – thou art a villain.

ROMEO Tybalt, the reason that I have to love thee
Doth much excuse the appertaining rage
To such a greeting. Villain am I none.
Therefore farewell, I see thou knowest me not.

TYBALT Boy, this shall not excuse the injuries
That thou hast done me, therefore turn and
draw.

ROMEO I do protest I never injured thee,   70
But love thee better than thou canst devise,
Till thou shalt know the reason of my love.
And so good Capulet, which name I tender
As dearly as my own, be satisfied.

MERCUTIO O calm, dishonourable, vile submission!
Alla stoccata carries it away.
Tybalt, you rat-catcher, will you walk?

TYBALT What wouldst thou have with me?

MERCUTIO Good King of Cats, nothing but one of
your nine lives, that I mean to make bold withal,   80
and, as you shall use me hereafter, dry-beat the rest
of the eight. Will you pluck your sword out of his
pilcher by the ears? Make haste, lest mine be about
your ears ere it be out.

TYBALT I am for you.

ROMEO Gentle Mercutio, put thy rapier up.

MERCUTIO Come sir, your *passado*.

ROMEO Draw Benvolio, beat down their weapons.
Gentlemen, for shame, forbear this outrage.
Tybalt, Mercutio, the Prince expressly hath   90
Forbid this bandying in Verona streets.
Hold Tybalt. Good Mercutio.

TYBALT *under* ROMEO'S *arm, wounds* MERCUTIO

A FOLLOWER Away, Tybalt!

[*Exit* TYBALT *with* FOLLOWERS

[94] A . . . houses *Mercutio's repeated dying curse on both Capulets and Montagues is fulfilled, even though, ironically, it is he who precipitated the tragic events which now follow.*

    sped *done for*

[95] and . . . nothing *without even a wound*

[96] a scratch *i.e. from the cat – but his subsequent words reveal that he knows he is fatally wounded.*

[97] villain *boy (with no derogatory sense)*

[99–100] No . . . serve *said with bitterness in response to Romeo's useless attempt to reassure him*

[100] serve *be enough – to kill him*

[101] grave *dead, very serious. Even at the moment of death Shakespeare's characters pun, but the Elizabethan attitude to word-play was different from ours.*

[102] peppered *finished*

[105–6] by . . . arithmetic *according to the book of rules. This is just what Tybalt did not do.*

[107] I . . . arm *Mercutio blames Romeo for his death as Romeo's intervention hid Tybalt's fatal thrust.*

[108] I thought . . . best *perhaps the most pathetic line in the play*

[111] worms' meat *food for worms*

    it *my death-blow*

[112] soundly *thoroughly*

[113] ally *relative*

[114] very *true*

[116] With . . . slander *By Tybalt's insult*

[117] cousin *relative (by marriage)*

[119] And in . . . steel *And softened the courageous part of my character*

MERCUTIO   I am hurt.
    A plague o' both houses! I am sped.
    Is he gone and hath nothing?
BENVOLIO   What, art thou hurt?
MERCUTIO Ay, ay, a scratch, a scratch; marry 'tis
    enough.
    Where is my page? Go villain, fetch a surgeon.
                      [*Exit* PAGE

ROMEO Courage man, the hurt cannot be much.
MERCUTIO No, 'tis not so deep as a well, nor so wide
    as a church-door; but 'tis enough, 'twill serve. Ask 100
    for me tomorrow, and you shall find me a grave
    man. I am peppered, I warrant, for this world. A
    plague o' both your houses! Zounds, a dog, a rat,
    a mouse, a cat, to scratch a man to death! A
    braggart, a rogue, a villain, that fights by the book
    of arithmetic! Why the devil came you between
    us? I was hurt under your arm.
ROMEO I thought all for the best.
MERCUTIO Help me into some house Benvolio,
    Or I shall faint. A plague o' both your houses! 110
    They have made worms' meat of me. I have
      it,
    And soundly too. Your houses!
               [*Exeunt* MERCUTIO *and* BENVOLIO
ROMEO This gentleman, the Prince's near ally,
    My very friend, hath got this mortal hurt
    In my behalf; my reputation stained
    With Tybalt's slander – Tybalt that an hour
    Hath been my cousin. O sweet Juliet,
    Thy beauty hath made me effeminate,
    And in my temper softened valour's steel.

Enter BENVOLIO

BENVOLIO O Romeo, Romeo, brave Mercutio is dead. 120

[121] aspired *soared up to*

[122] Which . . . earth *Which tragically early left the earth which he scorned. (But there could be a suggestion that the brave and characterful Mercutio arrived on earth before it was ready for him.)*

[123] This . . . depend *This day's misfortunes hang threateningly over more days to come*

[127] respective lenity *mercy that pays respect – to such matters as his new relationship with Tybalt*

[128] conduct *guide*

[135] This *My sword*

[137] up *aroused*

[138] amazed *dazed*
      doom thee *condemn you to*

[139] taken *captured*

[140] fortune's fool *the plaything (or dupe) of fortune. Is he?*

That gallant spirit hath aspired the clouds,
Which too untimely here did scorn the earth.

ROMEO This day's black fate on moe days doth
depend,
This but begins the woe others must end.

Enter TYBALT

BENVOLIO Here comes the furious Tybalt back again.

ROMEO Alive, in triumph, and Mercutio slain!
Away to heaven respective lenity,
And fire-eyed fury be my conduct now.
Now Tybalt take the 'villain' back again
That late thou gavest me, for Mercutio's soul 130
Is but a little way above our heads,
Staying for thine to keep him company.
Either thou or I, or both, must go with him.

TYBALT Thou wretched boy, that didst consort him
here,
Shalt with him hence.

ROMEO   This shall determine that.

They fight. TYBALT *falls*

BENVOLIO Romeo away, be gone.
The citizens are up, and Tybalt slain.
Stand not amazed, the Prince will doom
thee death
If thou art taken. Hence, be gone, away.

ROMEO O I am fortune's fool!

BENVOLIO   Why dost thou stay? 140
                              [*Exit* ROMEO

Enter CITIZENS

CITIZEN Which way ran he that killed Mercutio?
Tybalt, that murderer, which way ran he?

BENVOLIO There lies that Tybalt.

131

[143] **Up sir** *Shakespeare tells us that Benvolio should be kneeling by Tybalt's body.*

[146] **discover** *reveal*
[147] **manage** *course*

[150] **Tybalt . . . cousin** *Lady Capulet's emphasis on her relatives is made ironic by her not knowing that Romeo is her son-in-law. She now emerges as a character as full of hate as her nephew, Tybalt.*

[157] **spoke him fair** *spoke pleasantly to him*
[158] **nice** *trivial*
    urged withal *argued in addition*

[161] **Could . . . spleen** *Could not pacify the uncontrollable anger*
[162] **tilts** *thrusts*
[164] **all as hot** *just as angry*
[165] **with one . . .** *They probably fought with a rapier in one hand and a dagger in the other.*

[168] **Retorts it** *Returns it*

CITIZEN   Up sir, go with me;
I charge thee in the Prince's name obey.

Enter PRINCE, MONTAGUE, CAPULET, *their Wives and all*

PRINCE Where are the vile beginners of this fray?
BENVOLIO O noble Prince, I can discover all
    The unlucky manage of this fatal brawl.
    There lies the man, slain by young Romeo,
    That slew thy kinsman, brave Mercutio.
LADY CAPULET Tybalt, my cousin. O my brother's
    child!   150
    O Prince! O husband! O the blood is spilled
    Of my dear kinsman! Prince, as thou art true,
    For blood of ours shed blood of Montague.
    O cousin, cousin!
PRINCE Benvolio, who began this bloody fray?
BENVOLIO Tybalt here slain, whom Romeo's hand did
    slay.
    Romeo, that spoke him fair, bade him bethink
    How nice the quarrel was, and urged withal
    Your high displeasure. All this – utterèd
    With gentle breath, calm look, knees humbly
    bowed –   160
    Could not take truce with the unruly spleen
    Of Tybalt deaf to peace, but that he tilts
    With piercing steel at bold Mercutio's breast,
    Who, all as hot, turns deadly point to point,
    And with a martial scorn, with one hand beats
    Cold death aside, and with the other sends
    It back to Tybalt, whose dexterity
    Retorts it. Romeo he cries aloud,
    'Hold friends, friends part!' And swifter
    than his tongue,
    His agile arm beats down their fatal points,   170
    And 'twixt them rushes; underneath whose
    arm

[172] envious *malicious*
       hit the life *fatally wounded*
[173] stout *brave*
[174] by and by *immediately*
[175] newly . . . revenge *only then allowed thoughts of revenge to possess him*
[177] stout *Why does he call Tybalt brave?*

[181] Affection *Natural sympathy for the Montagues. Is Benvolio's description accurate?*

[187] Who . . . owe? *Who now is to pay the price of shedding the dear blood of Mercutio?*

[189–90] His . . . Tybalt *All that Romeo has done is execute the sentence of death on Tybalt which the law was bound to decree*

[192] I . . . interest *I am involved*
[193] My blood *i.e. the blood of Mercutio, his kinsman*
[194] amerce *punish*

[197] purchase out abuses *buy pardon for crimes*

An envious thrust from Tybalt hit the life
Of stout Mercutio, and then Tybalt fled;
But by and by comes back to Romeo,
Who had but newly entertained revenge,
And to it they go like lightning, for ere I
Could draw to part them, was stout Tybalt
    slain,
And as he fell, did Romeo turn and fly.
This is the truth, or let Benvolio die.

LADY CAPULET He is a kinsman to the Montague;   180
Affection makes him false, he speaks not true.
Some twenty of them fought in this black
    strife,
And all those twenty could but kill one life.
I beg for justice, which thou, Prince, must
    give.
Romeo slew Tybalt, Romeo must not live.

PRINCE Romeo slew him, he slew Mercutio.
Who now the price of his dear blood doth
    owe?

MONTAGUE Not Romeo, Prince, he was Mercutio's
    friend;
His fault concludes but what the law should
    end –
The life of Tybalt.

PRINCE   And for that offence   190
Immediately we do exile him hence.
I have an interest in your hate's proceeding;
My blood for your rude brawls doth lie a-
    bleeding.
But I'll amerce you with so strong a fine
That you shall all repent the loss of mine.
I will be deaf to pleading and excuses,
Nor tears nor prayers shall purchase out
    abuses.
Therefore use none. Let Romeo hence in haste,
Else, when he is found, that hour is his last.

[201] Mercy . . . kill *Mercy that pardons murderers only leads to further murders*

ACT THREE, scene 2

Yet another striking contrast – from violence and hatred in the streets to the passionate love of Juliet waiting in Capulet's house for her wedding-night. The dramatic irony is intense as the audience knows that her husband has been banished and her happiness will be short-lived.

[1] apace *swiftly*

fiery-footed steeds *the horses which draw the chariot of Phoebus, the sun-god. Juliet is longing for day to end.*

[3] Phaëton *Phoebus's son. Allowed to drive his father's chariot for one day, he lost control and was destroyed by a thunderbolt from Jupiter.*

[5] close *i.e. providing secrecy*

love-performing night *i.e. night that is made for the consummation of love*

[6] runaways' *possibly the horses allowed to run away by Phaëton*

[10] It . . . night *Because the darkness of night makes one blind*
civil *serious*

[12] learn *teach*

lose . . . match *She will lose her virginity but gain a husband.*

[14] Hood . . . cheeks *Cover with your black cloak my blushes fluttering in my cheeks. Juliet's innocence is repeatedly emphasised. The Nurse has already mentioned her blushing at II. 5. 71. The imagery is from hawking. An unmanned (untrained) falcon was trained by covering its head with a hood. Juliet is unmanned as she is a virgin. The fluttering of the falcon's wings was known as 'bating'.*

[15] strange *shy*

[16] Think . . . modesty *Think the physical consummation of true love as no more than simple modesty. Juliet's frank sensuality was so shocking to the Victorians that this speech was often omitted.*

[17] day in night *Romeo will make the night as bright as day.*

[22] stars *The imagery of this speech should be compared with that at the beginning of II. 2.*

[25] garish *gaudy*

Bear hence this body, and attend our will.   200
Mercy but murders, pardoning those that kill.
                              [*Exeunt*

Scene 2. *Enter* JULIET

JULIET Gallop apace, you fiery-footed steeds,
         Towards Phoebus' lodging; such a wagoner
         As Phaëton would whip you to the west,
         And bring in cloudy night immediately.
         Spread thy close curtain, love-performing
            night,
         That runaways' eyes may wink, and Romeo
         Leap to these arms, untalked of and unseen.
         Lovers can see to do their amorous rites
         By their own beauties; or if love be blind,
         It best agrees with night. Come civil night,   10
         Thou sober-suited matron all in black,
         And learn me how to lose a winning match,
         Played for a pair of stainless maidenhoods.
         Hood my unmanned blood, bating in my
            cheeks,
         With thy black mantle, till strange love grow
            bold,
         Think true love acted simple modesty.
         Come night, come Romeo, come thou day in
            night;
         For thou wilt lie upon the wings of night,
         Whiter than snow upon a raven's back.
         Come gentle night, come loving black-browed
            night,   20
         Give me my Romeo, and when he shall die,
         Take him and cut him out in little stars,
         And he will make the face of heaven so fine
         That all the world will be in love with night
         And pay no worship to the garish sun.

[34] cords *the rope ladder which was to bring Romeo to Juliet on their wedding night*

[37] weraday *well-a-day, alas*
[38] undone *ruined*

[40] envious *malicious*
    Romeo can *The Nurse is again unable to tell Juliet in a straightforward manner what has happened.*

[45–50] Say . . . 'no' *The repeated punning on 'Ay', 'I' and 'eye' is more acceptable if an audience knows that to the Elizabethans a pun was not just something comic. The ambiguity of a pun could add richness to a tragic moment. Is there any justification for it here?*
[46] 'I' *In Shakespeare's time 'Ay' was usually spelt as 'I'.*
[47] cockatrice *a legendary creature, hatched from a cock's egg by a serpent, and able to kill by its look*
[48] I . . . 'I' *I am not myself*
[49] those eyes *i.e. Romeo's eyes*
[51] Brief . . . woe *Sounds as short as 'Ay' or 'No' will decide whether I am to be happy or miserable*

O I have bought the mansion of a love,
But not possessed it, and, though I am sold,
Not yet enjoyed. So tedious is this day
As is the night before some festival
To an impatient child that hath new robes   30
And may not wear them. O here comes my
    Nurse,

Enter NURSE

And she brings news, and every tongue that
    speaks
But Romeo's name speaks heavenly eloquence.
Now Nurse, what news? What hast thou there?
    The cords
That Romeo bid thee fetch?

NURSE   Ay, ay, the cords.

JULIET Ay me, what news? Why dost thou wring thy
    hands?

NURSE Ah weraday, he's dead, he's dead, he's dead!
We are undone lady, we are undone.
Alack the day, he's gone, he's killed, he's dead!

JULIET Can heaven be so envious?

NURSE   Romeo can,   40
Though heaven cannot. O Romeo, Romeo,
Who ever would have thought it? Romeo!

JULIET What devil art thou that dost torment me thus?
This torture should be roared in dismal hell.
Hath Romeo slain himself? Say thou but 'Ay',
And that bare vowel 'I' shall poison more
Than the death-darting eye of cockatrice.
I am not I, if there should be such an 'I';
Or those eyes shut, that make thee answer
    'Ay'.
If he be slain, say 'Ay'; or if not, 'no'.   50
Brief sounds determine of my weal or woe.

NURSE I saw the wound, I saw it with mine eyes –

[53] God . . . mark   *May God forgive me for mentioning it*

[54] corse   *corpse*

[56] gore-blood   *congealed blood*
swoundèd   *fainted*

[57] bankrupt   *because in losing Romeo she has lost all her wealth*
. break   *die, go bankrupt*

[59] Vile . . . resign   *Vile body, yield yourself up to the grave*

[60] And . . . bier   *And may I and Romeo be buried in one tomb.*
Another ironic reference to the end of the play.

[61-2] O Tybalt . . . gentleman   *The Nurse's description of*
Tybalt is exaggerated and is not borne out by what the audience has
seen of him.

[64] What . . . contrary?   *Juliet is confused. Until now she*
thought that it was Romeo who was dead.

[67] dreadful trumpet   *A reference to the trumpet which will*
sound when the world ends and the last judgement takes place. See I
Corinthians 15. 52.

[73-85] O serpent . . . palace!   *The stream of oxymorons re-*
minds us of Romeo's speech at I. 1. 178, but there it was meant to be
artificial and mannered. What is the effect here?

[73] O serpent . . . face!   *Professor T. J. B. Spencer has pointed*
out that sometimes in pictures the Serpent in Paradise (Satan) was
shown as appearing to Eve with a human face surrounded by flowers.

[74] dragon . . . cave   *Dragons were believed to guard (keep)*
treasure in caves.

[76] wolvish . . . lamb   *looking like a lamb but as ravenous as a*
wolf

[78] Just   *The exact*
justly   *truly*

[81] bower   *enclose*

[81-2] When . . . flesh?   *The Garden of Eden is again in Juliet's*
thoughts.

[83-4] Was . . . bound?   *Juliet has heard her mother use similar*
imagery in describing Paris – see I. 3. 81-92.

God save the mark – here on his manly breast.
A piteous corse, a bloody piteous corse,
Pale, pale as ashes, all bedaubed in blood,
All in gore-blood. I swoundèd at the sight.

JULIET O break, my heart, poor bankrupt, break at
  once!
To prison eyes, ne'er look on liberty.
Vile earth, to earth resign; end motion here,
And thou and Romeo press one heavy bier.   60

NURSE O Tybalt, Tybalt, the best friend I had,
O courteous Tybalt, honest gentleman,
That ever I should live to see thee dead!

JULIET What storm is this that blows so contrary?
Is Romeo slaughtered? And is Tybalt dead?
My dearest cousin, and my dearer lord?
Then dreadful trumpet, sound the general
  doom,
For who is living, if those two are gone?

NURSE Tybalt is gone, and Romeo banishèd.
Romeo that killed him, he is banishèd.   70

JULIET O God, did Romeo's hand shed Tybalt's blood?

NURSE It did, it did, alas the day, it did!

JULIET O serpent heart, hid with a flow'ring face!
Did ever dragon keep so fair a cave?
Beautiful tyrant, fiend angelical,
Dove-feathered raven, wolvish ravening lamb,
Despisèd substance of divinest show,
Just opposite to what thou justly seem'st,
A damnèd saint, an honourable villain!
O nature, what hadst thou to do in hell   80
When thou didst bower the spirit of a fiend
In mortal paradise of such sweet flesh?
Was ever book containing such vile matter
So fairly bound? O that deceit should dwell
In such a gorgeous palace!

NURSE   There's no trust,
No faith, no honesty in men; all perjured,

141

[87] naught   *wicked*
    dissemblers   *hypocrites*
[88] aqua vitae   *brandy or other strong spirits. The Nurse likes her drink. The cry goes up again at IV. 5. 16!*
[89] griefs . . . woes . . . sorrows   *The Nurse never says in one word what she can say in three.*

[90] Blistered   *Juliet realises that her real feelings are with her husband and flies to his defence when the Nurse attacks him.*

[98] poor my   *my poor*
    smooth   *speak well of*
[99] three-hours wife   *another reminder of the speed at which events are happening*
    mangled   *i.e. in her speech beginning 'O serpent heart', and with an obvious antithesis to the literal sense of 'smooth'*

[102] native spring   *source*
[103-4] Your . . . joy   *Your drops should be offered up as a tribute to woe but you are mistakenly offering them up to joy*

[109] fain   *gladly*

[111] Like . . . minds   *Like the memory in the conscience of sinners of guilty deeds which will damn them to hell*

All forsworn, all naught, all dissemblers.
Ah, where's my man? Give me some aqua
vitae.
These griefs, these woes, these sorrows make
me old.
Shame come to Romeo!

JULIET   Blistered be thy tongue   90
For such a wish. He was not born to shame.
Upon his brow shame is ashamed to sit;
For 'tis a throne where honour may be crowned
Sole monarch of the universal earth.
O what a beast was I to chide at him!

NURSE Will you speak well of him that killed your
cousin?

JULIET Shall I speak ill of him that is my husband?
Ah poor my lord, what tongue shall smooth
thy name
When I thy three-hours wife have mangled
it?
But wherefore, villain, didst thou kill my
cousin?   100
That villain cousin would have killed my
husband.
Back foolish tears, back to your native spring.
Your tributary drops belong to woe,
Which you, mistaking, offer up to joy.
My husband lives, that Tybalt would have
slain,
And Tybalt's dead, that would have slain my
husband.
All this is comfort, wherefore weep I then?
Some word there was, worser than Tybalt's
death,
That murdered me. I would forget it fain;
But O, it presses to my memory,   110
Like damnèd guilty deeds to sinners' minds –
'Tybalt is dead, and Romeo banishèd.'

143

[114] hath . . . Tybalts *is as bad as the death of ten thousand Tybalts*

[117] needly . . . ranked *must necessarily be accompanied. (Compare in* Hamlet, *'When sorrows come, they come not single spies/But in battalions'.)*

[120] Which . . . moved? *which might have resulted in an ordinary grief – because the deaths of mother and father may be expected, unlike the banishment of Romeo*

[121] But . . . death *But to follow up, as if with some rearguard (with a pun on 'last word'), the news of Tybalt's death*

[126] that . . . death *the death implied in that word*
   that woe sound *measure the depth of that sorrow, express that sorrow*

[132] beguiled *cheated*

[135] maiden-widowèd *widowed without ever really being a wife*

[139] wot *know*

That 'banishèd', that one word 'banishèd',
Hath slain ten thousand Tybalts. Tybalt's
death
Was woe enough if it had ended there.
Or if sour woe delights in fellowship
And needly will be ranked with other griefs,
Why followed not, when she said 'Tybalt's
dead',
'Thy father', or 'thy mother', nay, or both,
Which modern lamentation might have
moved?   120
But with a rear-ward following Tybalt's
death,
'Romeo is banishèd' – to speak that word
Is father, mother, Tybalt, Romeo, Juliet,
All slain, all dead. 'Romeo is banishèd.'
There is no end, no limit, measure, bound,
In that word's death; no words can that woe
sound.
Where is my father and my mother, Nurse?
NURSE Weeping and wailing over Tybalt's corse.
Will you go to them? I will bring you thither.
JULIET Wash they his wounds with tears? Mine shall
be spent,   130
When theirs are dry, for Romeo's banishment.
Take up those cords. Poor ropes you are
beguiled,
Both you and I, for Romeo is exiled.
He made you for a highway to my bed,
But I, a maid, die maiden-widowèd.
Come cords, come Nurse, I'll to my wedding-
bed,
And death, not Romeo, take my maidenhead.
NURSE Hie to your chamber. I'll find Romeo
To comfort you. I wot well where he is.
Hark ye, your Romeo will be here at night.   140
I'll to him; he is hid at Lawrence' cell.

ACT THREE, scene 3

The Nurse has just mentioned the Friar's cell, and in this way Shakespeare has subtly told us where we shall be next. The audience has seen Juliet's reaction to the news of banishment, now it can compare Romeo's. Does the play flag here because of Shakespeare's immaturity, or is he telling us something of value about Romeo's character? Is Granville-Barker right in saying that there is no relaxation in tension, vehemence or speed? The contrast now is between the philosophic Friar and the 'feeling' Romeo.

[1] fearful *frightened*
[2] Affliction . . . parts *Suffering has fallen in love with your personal qualities*
[3] thou . . . calamity *Just as Juliet is married to death, Romeo is married to calamity.*
[4] doom *judgement*
[6] familiar *closely associated*
[8] tidings *news*
[9] doomsday *death (literally the Day of Judgement)*
[10] vanished *This could mean 'escaped', but 'vanished' may be textually corrupt and may originally have been 'banished'.*
[11] banishment *As in the previous scene, a pattern of sound is made out of 'banishment' and 'banishèd'.*

[17] without *outside*
[19] banished . . . world *because Verona is Romeo's whole world while Juliet lives there*

JULIET O find him, give this ring to my true knight,
And bid him come to take his last farewell.

[*Exeunt*

Scene 3. *Enter* FRIAR LAWRENCE

FRIAR LAWRENCE Romeo, come forth, come forth thou
fearful man.
Affliction is enamoured of thy parts,
And thou art wedded to calamity.

Enter ROMEO

ROMEO Father, what news? What is the Prince's
doom?
What sorrow craves acquaintance at my hand,
That I yet know not.
FRIAR LAWRENCE   Too familiar
Is my dear son with such sour company.
I bring thee tidings of the Prince's doom.
ROMEO What less than doomsday is the Prince's
doom?
FRIAR LAWRENCE A gentler judgement vanished from
his lips,   10
Not body's death, but body's banishment.
ROMEO Ha, banishment? Be merciful, say 'death';
For exile hath more terror in his look,
Much more than death. Do not say 'banish-
ment'.
FRIAR LAWRENCE Hence from Verona art thou
banishèd.
Be patient, for the world is broad and wide.
ROMEO There is no world without Verona walls,
But purgatory, torture, hell itself.
Hence banishèd is banished from the world,

147

[20] world's exile   *exile from the world*

[21-3] Calling . . . me   *Romeo protests that as banishment from Juliet means death to him, it is useless to make out that it is something better. The use of a golden axe doesn't make death more acceptable.*

[24] O . . . sin!   *i.e. Romeo's ingratitude*

[25] fault   *crime*

[26] part   *side*
       rushed aside   *put aside – but 'rushed' could be a textual error for 'pushed'*
[28] dear   *unusual*

[33] validity   *value*
[34] state   *rank or status*
       courtship   *courtly behaviour, wooing*
[35] carrion   *that feed on dead flesh*
[36-7] On . . . lips   *The movement is from Juliet's hands to her lips, as at I. 5. 94-7.*
[38] vestal   *chaste*
[39] Still . . . sin   *Her lips always blush – as if it were a sin – when they touch each other*

[44] poison   *Shakespeare reminds us of the Friar's knowledge of drugs and again makes ominous mention of suicide.*
[45] sudden mean   *swift means*
       though . . . mean   *no matter how ignoble*
[47] damnèd . . . hell   *because they are banished from God's presence*
[48] Howling . . . it   *The wailing (of the damned) is heard with that word*
[49] divine   *priest*
       ghostly confessor   *holy hearer of confession*
[51] mangle   *lacerate. Juliet uses 'mangled' in the previous scene. Romeo's speeches now echo hers.*

And world's exile is death. Then 'banishèd'   20
Is death mis-termed. Calling death 'banishèd',
Thou cut'st my head off with a golden axe,
And smilest upon the stroke that murders me.

FRIAR LAWRENCE O deadly sin! O rude unthankful-
    ness!
    Thy fault our law calls death, but the kind
    Prince
    Taking thy part hath rushed aside the law,
    And turned that black word 'death' to 'banish-
    ment'.
    This is dear mercy, and thou seest it not.

ROMEO 'Tis torture and not mercy. Heaven is here
    Where Juliet lives, and every cat and dog,   30
    And little mouse, every unworthy thing,
    Live here in heaven and may look on her,
    But Romeo may not. More validity,
    More honourable state, more courtship lives
    In carrion flies than Romeo. They may seize
    On the white wonder of dear Juliet's hand,
    And steal immortal blessing from her lips,
    Who even in pure and vestal modesty
    Still blush, as thinking their own kisses sin.
    But Romeo may not, he is banishèd.   40
    Flies may do this, but I from this must fly;
    They are free men, but I am banishèd.
    And say'st thou yet that exile is not death?
    Hadst thou no poison mixed, no sharp-ground
    knife,
    No sudden mean of death, though ne'er so
    mean,
    But 'banishèd' to kill me? Banishèd!
    O friar, the damnèd use that word in hell;
    Howling attends it. How hast thou the heart,
    Being a divine, a ghostly confessor,
    A sin-absolver, and my friend professed,   50
    To mangle me with that word banishèd?

[52] fond   *foolish*

[57] Yet 'banishèd'   *Must you keep saying 'banishèd'?*
Hang up   *Hang*
[59] Displant   *Uproot*
[60] prevails not   *has no effect*

[62] have no eyes   *i.e. to see what is obvious*

[63] dispute . . . estate   *discuss sensibly your affairs with you*

[67] Doting   *Madly in love*

[70] Taking . . . grave   *Romeo lies on the ground as if measuring out his own grave.*

[75] taken   *captured*

FRIAR LAWRENCE Thou fond mad man, hear me a little
    speak.
ROMEO O thou wilt speak again of banishment.
FRIAR LAWRENCE I'll give thee armour to keep off that
    word –
    Adversity's sweet milk, philosophy,
    To comfort thee though thou art banishèd.
ROMEO Yet 'banishèd'? Hang up philosophy!
    Unless philosophy can make a Juliet,
    Displant a town, reverse a prince's doom,
    It helps not, it prevails not. Talk no more.   60
FRIAR LAWRENCE O then I see that madmen have no
    ears.
ROMEO How should they when that wise men have no
    eyes?
FRIAR LAWRENCE Let me dispute with thee of thy
    estate.
ROMEO Thou canst not speak of that thou dost not
    feel.
    Wert thou as young as I, Juliet thy love,
    An hour but married, Tybalt murderèd,
    Doting like me, and like me banishèd,
    Then mightst thou speak, then mightst thou
    tear thy hair,
    And fall upon the ground, as I do now,
    Taking the measure of an unmade grave.   70

NURSE *knocks*

FRIAR LAWRENCE Arise; one knocks; good Romeo
    hide thyself.
ROMEO Not I, unless the breath of heart-sick groans
    Mist-like enfold me from the search of eyes.

NURSE *knocks*

FRIAR LAWRENCE Hark how they knock! – Who's
    there? – Romeo arise;
    Thou wilt be taken – Stay awhile – Stand up.

[77] simpleness *folly. Romeo still does not hide himself.*

[83] with . . . drunk *The Friar's annoyance comes powerfully through this memorable image.*

[84–90] O . . . an O? *The Nurse's speech contains more bawdry. Shakespeare's command of his craft was such that he does not hesitate to bring comedy into serious scenes.*

[84] even . . . case *in exactly the same state as my mistress*

[85] woeful sympathy *They are partners in grief.*

[87] Blubbering *Wailing*

[88] an *if*

[90] an O *a moan of sorrow*

[93] old *experienced*

[95] blood . . . own *i.e. the blood of Tybalt, her kinsman*

[97] concealed lady *secret wife*
    cancelled *annulled*

[98] O she . . . weeps *The audience knows that the Nurse is inaccurate and exaggerates.*

[100] on . . . cries *cries out against Romeo*

NURSE *knocks*

Run to my study – By and by – God's will,
What simpleness is this? – I come, I come.

NURSE *knocks*

Who knocks so hard? Whence come you?
    What's your will?
NURSE [*Within*] Let me come in, and you shall know
    my errand.
    I come from Lady Juliet.
FRIAR LAWRENCE   Welcome then.   80
NURSE O holy friar, O tell me holy friar,
    Where is my lady's lord? Where's Romeo?
FRIAR LAWRENCE There on the ground, with his own
    tears made drunk.
NURSE O he is even in my mistress' case,
    Just in her case. O woeful sympathy,
    Piteous predicament! Even so lies she,
    Blubbering and weeping, weeping and
    blubbering.
    Stand up, stand up; stand an you be a man.
    For Juliet's sake, for her sake rise and stand.
    Why should you fall into so deep an O?   90
ROMEO Nurse –
NURSE   Ah sir, ah sir, death's the end of all.
ROMEO Spakest thou of Juliet? How is it with her?
    Doth not she think me an old murderer,
    Now I have stained the childhood of our joy
    With blood removed but little from her own?
    Where is she? And how doth she? And what
    says
    My concealed lady to our cancelled love?
NURSE O she says nothing sir, but weeps and weeps,
    And now falls on her bed, and then starts up,
    And Tybalt calls, and then on Romeo cries,   100
    And then down falls again.

[102] level *aim*

[105] anatomy *wretched body*
[106–7] sack . . . mansion *ransack my hateful body to find it (my name). Compare II. 2. 55–7 where he previously threatened violence to his name.*
[107] hateful mansion *This attempt at suicide is yet further preparing of the audience for Romeo's suicide when it comes.*

[108] form *appearance*

[111–12] Unseemly . . . both *You seem like a man but behave like an unnatural woman, and in being like both man and woman at once you resemble some monstrous beast*
[113] my holy order *i.e. of St Francis*
[114] tempered *balanced in its qualities*

[116] in . . . lives *lives only for you*
[117] damnèd *Suicide was a mortal sin and led to damnation in hell.*
[118] rail'st . . . on *do you abuse*
      birth . . . earth *family origin, soul and body*

[120] wouldst lose *i.e. by committing suicide*

[121–3] thou . . . indeed *You are well supplied with looks, affection and intelligence but put these qualities to shame by misusing them as a money-lender does his wealth*

[125] form of wax *a mere wax figure*
[126] Digressing . . . man *If you depart from the courage we associate with a man*

154

ROMEO   As if that name,
Shot from the deadly level of a gun,
Did murder her, as that name's cursèd hand
Murdered her kinsman. O tell me friar, tell
    me,
In what vile part of this anatomy
Doth my name lodge? Tell me, that I may
    sack
The hateful mansion.

He offers to stab himself and the NURSE *snatches the
                    dagger away*

FRIAR LAWRENCE   Hold thy desperate hand.
Art thou a man? Thy form cries out thou art.
Thy tears are womanish, thy wild acts denote   110
The unreasonable fury of a beast.
Unseemly woman in a seeming man,
And ill-beseeming beast in seeming both,
Thou hast amazed me. By my holy order,
I thought thy disposition better tempered.
Hast thou slain Tybalt? Wilt thou slay thyself,
And slay thy lady that in thy life lives,
By doing damnèd hate upon thyself?
Why rail'st thou on thy birth, the heaven, and
    earth,
Since birth, and heaven, and earth, all three
    do meet
In thee at once, which thou at once wouldst
    lose?   120
Fie, fie, thou sham'st thy shape, thy love, thy
    wit,
Which like a usurer abound'st in all,
And usest none in that true use indeed
Which should bedeck thy shape, thy love, thy
    wit.
Thy noble shape is but a form of wax,
Digressing from the valour of a man;

[127] but hollow perjury *is no more than an empty lie*
[128] Killing *If you kill*

[129-33] Thy ... defence *Your intelligence, which should embellish your body and love, fails properly to guide either, and, like the powder in an untrained soldier's gunpowder-flask, is set on fire through your own ignorance and destroys you instead of protecting you*

[135] lately dead *recently declaring yourself dead*
[136, 137 and 139] happy *fortunate*

[140] light *alight*
[141] Happiness *Good fortune*

[143] pouts *looks with displeasure*
    fortune *good fortune*
[145] decreed *decided*
[146] Ascend *Climb up to*
[147] watch be set *watchmen are posted at the city gates*

[150] blaze *make public*

[156] apt unto *ready to do*

[158-9] O Lord ... is! *The Nurse's stupefaction at the Friar's wisdom overwhelms her and brings us back to earth!*

Thy dear love sworn but hollow perjury,
Killing that love which thou hast vowed to
    cherish.
Thy wit, that ornament to shape and love,
Misshapen in the conduct of them both,   130
Like powder in a skilless soldier's flask
Is set afire by thine own ignorance,
And thou dismembered with thine own
    defence.
What, rouse thee man, thy Juliet is alive,
For whose dear sake thou wast but lately dead.
There art thou happy. Tybalt would kill thee,
But thou slewest Tybalt; there art thou happy.
The law that threatened death becomes thy
    friend,
And turns it to exile; there art thou happy.
A pack of blessings light upon thy back,   140
Happiness courts thee in her best array,
But, like a misbehaved and sullen wench,
Thou pouts upon thy fortune and thy love.
Take heed, take heed, for such die miserable.
Go get thee to thy love as was decreed,
Ascend her chamber, hence and comfort her.
But look thou stay not till the watch be set,
For then thou canst not pass to Mantua,
Where thou shalt live till we can find a time
To blaze your marriage, reconcile your
    friends,   150
Beg pardon of the Prince, and call thee back
With twenty hundred thousand times more joy
Than thou went'st forth in lamentation.
Go before, Nurse. Commend me to thy lady,
And bid her hasten all the house to bed,
Which heavy sorrow makes them apt unto.
Romeo is coming.
NURSE   O Lord, I could have stayed here all the night
    To hear good counsel. O what learning is!

[161] chide *scold*

[163] Hie *Hasten*

[164] comfort *happiness*

[165] here . . . state *your whole future prosperity depends on your observing what I say*

[166-7] Either . . . hence *The Friar had previously suggested (line 147) that Romeo should leave for Mantua before night. Now he offers the alternative of staying with Juliet till dawn, and then leaving Verona in disguise. It would not have been a valid marriage if it had not been consummated.*

[168] your man *i.e. Balthasar*

[170] good hap *piece of good fortune. Ironically it is Balthasar who brings the bad news.*

[172] a joy *i.e. the joy of seeing Juliet*

past . . . me *surpassing all other joys calls me away*

[173] It . . . thee *I should be unhappy to part from you so hastily*

ACT THREE, scene 4

The screw is turned and the lover's plight worsens. This supremely ironic scene, in which Capulet shrewdly decides to marry off his daughter to the Prince's wealthy kinsman, is acted on the main stage while, at the very same time, Juliet may be imagined as consummating her marriage to Romeo behind the curtains of the balcony on which the lovers will appear in the next scene. Capulet's unawareness of the real situation is paralleled by the lovers' unawareness of the new threat which hangs over them.

[1] fall'n out *happened*

[2] move *urge*

[4] Well . . . die *Capulet's easy philosophy reminds one of Romeo's 'Thou canst not speak of that thou dost not feel'.*

[6] promise *assure*

but for *if it had not been for*

My lord, I'll tell my lady you will come. 160
ROMEO Do so, and bid my sweet prepare to chide.
NURSE Here sir, a ring she bid me give you sir.
Hie you, make haste, for it grows very late.

[Exit

ROMEO How well my comfort is revived by this.
FRIAR LAWRENCE Go hence; good night; and here
stands all your state –
Either be gone before the watch be set,
Or by the break of day disguised from hence.
Sojourn in Mantua; I'll find out your man,
And he shall signify from time to time
Every good hap to you that chances here. 170
Give me thy hand, 'tis late. Farewell; good
night.
ROMEO But that a joy past joy calls out on me,
It were a grief so brief to part with thee.
Farewell.

[Exeunt

Scene 4. *Enter* CAPULET, LADY CAPULET *and* PARIS

CAPULET Things have fall'n out sir, so unluckily,
That we have had no time to move our
daughter.
Look you, she loved her kinsman Tybalt
dearly,
And so did I. Well, we were born to die.
'Tis very late, she'll not come down tonight.
I promise you, but for your company,
I would have been abed an hour ago.
PARIS These times of woe afford no times to woo.
Madam good night; commend me to your
daughter.
LADY CAPULET I will, and know her mind early
tomorrow; 10

159

[11] mewed ... heaviness *shut up with her sorrow (but with a strong secondary meaning for the audience)*

[12] make ... tender *be so bold as to make an offer*

[14] I ... not *His proud assumption of absolute power over his daughter explains his annoyance when he is crossed by her.*

[16] ear *This is Dover Wilson's inspired emendation of 'here' which had been accepted by most previous editors but is untypical of Shakespeare because of its meaninglessness.*

son *His certainty of Juliet's acceptance is such that he already calls Paris his 'son'.*

[17] Wednesday *Why the haste? Even Capulet at first thinks that it is too soon.*

[18] soft *a moment*

[19] Ha, ha *He is not laughing but thoughtful and would be saying 'h'm'.*

[20] A' *On*

[23] We'll ... ado *We won't have a big affair*

[24] late *recently*

[25] It ... thought *Capulet's behaviour depends upon what others think.*

we ... carelessly *we hadn't much respect for him*

[32] against *in time for*

[33] Light ... ho! *As Shakespeare's audience watched the play in a theatre open to the skies, he continually reminds them by devices such as this of the time of the play's action.*

[35] by and by *very soon*

Tonight she's mewed up to her heaviness.

PARIS *offers to go in and* CAPULET *calls him again*

CAPULET Sir Paris, I will make a desperate tender
Of my child's love. I think she will be ruled
In all respects by me; nay more, I doubt it
not.
Wife, go you to her ere you go to bed,
Acquaint her ear of my son Paris' love;
And bid her, mark you me, on Wednesday
next –
But soft, what day is this?

PARIS   Monday, my lord.

CAPULET Monday? Ha, ha, well Wednesday is too
soon;
A' Thursday let it be; a' Thursday, tell her,   20
She shall be married to this noble earl.
Will you be ready? Do you like this haste?
We'll keep no great ado – a friend or two –
For hark you, Tybalt being slain so late,
It may be thought we held him carelessly,
Being our kinsman, if we revel much.
Therefore we'll have some half a dozen friends,
And there an end. But what say you to
Thursday?

PARIS My lord, I would that Thursday were
tomorrow.

CAPULET Well, get you gone; a' Thursday be it then.   30
Go you to Juliet ere you go to bed;
Prepare her, wife, against this wedding-day.
Farewell my lord. Light to my chamber ho!
Afore me, it is so very late that we
May call it early by and by. Good night.

                                [*Exeunt*

ACT THREE, scene 5

*As the stage empties, Romeo and Juliet appear on the balcony.
The lyrical, poignant beauty of the opening makes even more
vicious Capulet's cruelty in trying to force an arranged marriage on to a Juliet who has just learned of the ecstasies of a
real marriage. There is contrast between the young lost in their
love for each other and the old lost in their insensitivity, self-
interest and concern for appearances. Juliet, rejected by those
who claim to love her, turns at the end of the scene to her last
hope, the Friar.*

[3] fearful *full of fear*
[4] pomegranate *pronounced 'pom'granate'*
[7] envious streaks *'Envious' was twice used in the first balcony
scene (II. 2) and its echo reminds us strongly of that earlier parting.*
[8] severing clouds *clouds which are breaking up and separate us*
[9] Night's candles *the stars*
  jocund *joyful*
[13] exhaled *drew forth. Vapours drawn up from the earth by the
sun and then ignited by its heat were supposed to cause meteors.*

[17] ta'en *taken, i.e. captured*

[19] morning's eye *sun*
[20] reflex . . . brow *reflection of the forehead of Cynthia (the
moon-goddess), i.e. it is but the reflection of the moon*
[22] vaulty *arched*
[23] care *desire ·*

[25] my soul *i.e. Juliet*

[28] sharps *high-pitched, shrill notes (of music)*
[29] division *melody – but Juliet puns on the sense of 'separation'*
[30] This *i.e. the lark*
[31] Some . . . eyes *As the toad's eyes were thought to be more
beautiful than the lark's it was a popular belief that they must have
changed eyes.*

Scene 5. *Enter* ROMEO *and* JULIET

JULIET Wilt thou be gone? It is not yet near day.
It was the nightingale, and not the lark,
That pierced the fearful hollow of thine ear.
Nightly she sings on yon pomegranate tree.
Believe me love, it was the nightingale.

ROMEO It was the lark, the herald of the morn,
No nightingale. Look love, what envious streaks
Do lace the severing clouds in yonder east.
Night's candles are burnt out, and jocund day
Stands tiptoe on the misty mountain tops.   10
I must be gone and live, or stay and die.

JULIET Yon light is not daylight; I know it, I.
It is some meteor that the sun exhaled
To be to thee this night a torch-bearer,
And light thee on thy way to Mantua.
Therefore stay yet, thou need'st not to be gone.

ROMEO Let me be ta'en, let me be put to death;
I am content, so thou wilt have it so.
I'll say yon gray is not the morning's eye,
'Tis but the pale reflex of Cynthia's brow.   20
Nor that is not the lark, whose notes do beat
The vaulty heaven so high above our heads.
I have more care to stay than will to go.
Come death, and welcome! Juliet wills it so.
How is't, my soul? Let's talk; it is not day.

JULIET It is, it is, hie hence, be gone, away.
It is the lark that sings so out of tune,
Straining harsh discords, and unpleasing sharps.
Some say the lark makes sweet division;
This doth not so, for she divideth us.   30
Some say the lark and loathèd toad changed eyes,

163

[32] had . . . too *because the croaking of the toad would have been more appropriate to our parting than the sweet song of the lark*

[33] Since . . . affray *Because that song of the lark is frightening us out of each other's arms*

[34] hunt's-up *a song used to awaken huntsmen and also newly-married couples*

[36] More . . . woes *The imagery of light and dark persists.*

[40] look about *be on the watch*

[41] life *i.e. Romeo*

[43] friend *sweetheart*

[46] count *way of counting*
much in years *very old*

[54] ill-divining soul *soul which sees misfortune ahead*

[55] so low *Romeo is climbing down the rope ladder.*

[56] As . . . tomb *Juliet next sees Romeo dead in a tomb.*

[57] Either . . . pale *As she looks down on him in the dawn light he might well look pale.*

[59] Dry . . . blood *Sighing was believed to use up the blood, and, thus, their sorrow at parting makes them look pale – i.e. bloodless.*

O now I would they had changed voices too,
Since arm from arm that voice doth us affray,
Hunting thee hence with hunt's-up to the day.
O now be gone; more light and light it grows.
ROMEO More light and light, more dark and dark our
    woes.

Enter NURSE *hastily*

NURSE Madam.
JULIET Nurse.
NURSE Your lady mother is coming to your chamber.
    The day is broke, be wary, look about.   40
                                             [*Exit*
JULIET Then window let day in, and let life out.
ROMEO Farewell, farewell. One kiss, and I'll descend.

He goes down

JULIET Art thou gone so, love, lord, ay husband,
    friend?
    I must hear from thee every day in the hour,
    For in a minute there are many days.
    O by this count I shall be much in years,
    Ere I again behold my Romeo.
ROMEO Farewell.
    I will omit no opportunity
    That may convey my greetings, love, to thee.   50
JULIET O think'st thou we shall ever meet again?
ROMEO I doubt it not, and all these woes shall serve
    For sweet discourses in our times to come.
JULIET O God, I have an ill-divining soul.
    Methinks I see thee now thou art so low,
    As one dead in the bottom of a tomb.
    Either my eyesight fails, or thou look'st pale.
ROMEO And trust me love, in my eye so do you.
    Dry sorrow drinks our blood. Adieu, adieu.
                                             [*Exit*

[60–2] O . . . faith? *The goddess, Fortune, is so fickle that Juliet wonders what interest she can have in someone so faithful as Romeo.*
She goes down . . . *This stage direction from the First Quarto suggests that at this point Juliet leaves the balcony by an inner staircase and appears on the main stage where the rest of the scene takes place.*

[66] Is . . . early *Is she very late in going to bed or early in getting up?*
[67] unaccustomed . . . procures *unusual reason brings*

[68] how now . . . ? *what's the matter?*

[72] some *a certain amount of*

[73] much . . . wit *an excess of sorrow always shows some deficiency of good sense*
[74] feeling *heartfelt. Juliet's following speeches have a double meaning which the audience understands but which is not apparent to her mother.*
[75–6] but . . . for *because no amount of weeping can bring Tybalt alive so that Juliet can feel him*

[78–9] Well . . . him *Lady Capulet assumes that Juliet shares her vengeful feelings.*

JULIET O Fortune, Fortune, all men call thee fickle; 60
   If thou art fickle, what does thou with him
   That is renowned for faith? Be fickle, Fortune;
   For then I hope thou wilt not keep him long,
   But send him back.

She goes down from the window

LADY CAPULET   Ho daughter, are you up?
JULIET Who is 't that calls? It is my lady mother.
   Is she not down so late, or up so early?
   What unaccustomed cause procures her hither?

Enter LADY CAPULET

LADY CAPULET Why, how now Juliet?
JULIET   Madam I am not well.
LADY CAPULET Evermore weeping for your cousin's
   death?
   What, wilt thou wash him from his grave with
   tears? 70
   An if thou couldst, thou couldst not make him
   live.
   Therefore have done; some grief shows much
   of love,
   But much of grief shows still some want of wit.
JULIET Yet let me weep for such a feeling loss.
LADY CAPULET So shall you feel the loss, but not the
   friend
   Which you weep for.
JULIET   Feeling so the loss,
   I cannot choose but ever weep the friend.
LADY CAPULET Well girl, thou weep'st not so much
   for his death,
   As that the villain lives which slaughtered him.
JULIET What villain, Madam?
LADY CAPULET   That same villain Romeo. 80
JULIET [*Aside*] Villain and he be many miles asunder –

167

[85] from . . . hands *Lady Capulet does not realise that Juliet means that she would like to caress Romeo with her hands.*

[86] venge *avenge*

[89] runagate *vagabond – but how does she know that Romeo is going to Mantua?*

[90] unaccustomed dram *unusual drink, i.e. a dose of poison. Lady Capulet savagely pours out her hatred not realising that it is her son-in-law she wishes to murder. Ironically he will die of an 'unaccustomed dram'.*

[94] dead *Juliet places the word so that it can apply to what has gone before or what comes after, thus confusing her mother.*

[97] temper *mix, weaken*

[99] sleep in quiet *die, sleep peacefully*

[101] wreak *give expression to*

[102] his body *i.e. Romeo's*

[105] needy *unhappy*

[107] careful *i.e. concerned for Juliet's welfare*

[109] sorted out *chosen*

[110] nor . . . not *This is an emphatic double negative. The negatives do not cancel themselves out.*

[*Aloud*] God pardon him; I do with all my
    heart;
And yet no man like he doth grieve my heart.

LADY CAPULET That is because the traitor murderer
    lives.

JULIET Ay madam, from the reach of these my hands.
    Would none but I might venge my cousin's
    death.

LADY CAPULET We will have vengeance for it, fear thou
    not.
    Then weep no more. I'll send to one in
    Mantua,
    Where that same banished runagate doth live,
    Shall give him such an unaccustomed dram   90
    That he shall soon keep Tybalt company;
    And then I hope thou wilt be satisfied.

JULIET Indeed I never shall be satisfied
    With Romeo, till I behold him – dead –
    Is my poor heart so for a kinsman vexed.
    Madam, if you could find out but a man
    To bear poison, I would temper it,
    That Romeo should upon receipt thereof
    Soon sleep in quiet. O how my heart abhors
    To hear him named – and cannot come to
    him –   100
    To wreak the love I bore my cousin
    Upon his body that hath slaughtered him.

LADY CAPULET Find thou the means, and I'll find such
    a man.
    But now I'll tell thee joyful tidings, girl.

JULIET And joy comes well in such a needy time.
    What are they, I beseech your ladyship?

LADY CAPULET Well, well, thou hast a careful father
    child,
    One who to put thee from thy heaviness
    Hath sorted out a sudden day of joy
    That thou expects not, nor I looked not for.   110

[111] in happy time   *it comes at a fortunate time*
[112] Marry   *By Mary*

[117] He ... bride   *Juliet's remarkable development is seen if her response now to the suggestion that she should marry Paris is compared with that in I. 3.*

[127] sunset   *death*

[129] conduit   *a fountain, sometimes shaped like a human figure. What is the effect of Capulet's tedious and over-ingenious imagery coming as it does immediately after Juliet's powerful outburst?*
[131] counterfeits   *imitates*
[132] still   *continually*

[135] they with them   *i.e. your tears raging with your sighs*

[136] Without   *Unless there comes*
        overset   *capsize*
[138] decree   *decision*

JULIET Madam, in happy time, what day is that?
LADY CAPULET Marry, my child, early next Thursday
    morn,
    The gallant, young, and noble gentleman,
    The County Paris, at St Peter's Church
    Shall happily make thee there a joyful bride.
JULIET Now by Saint Peter's Church, and Peter too,
    He shall not make me there a joyful bride.
    I wonder at this haste, that I must wed
    Ere he that should be husband comes to woo.
    I pray you tell my lord and father, madam,   120
    I will not marry yet, and when I do, I swear
    It shall be Romeo, whom you know I hate,
    Rather than Paris. These are news indeed.
LADY CAPULET Here comes your father; tell him so
    yourself,
    And see how he will take it at your hands.

Enter CAPULET *and* NURSE

CAPULET When the sun sets, the earth doth drizzle
    dew;
    But for the sunset of my brother's son
    It rains downright.
    How now, a conduit, girl? What, still in tears?
    Evermore showering? In one little body   130
    Thou counterfeits a bark, a sea, a wind,
    For still thy eyes, which I may call the sea,
    Do ebb and flow with tears; the bark thy body
    is,
    Sailing in this salt flood; the winds, thy
    sighs,
    Who, raging with thy tears, and they with
    them,
    Without a sudden calm, will overset
    Thy tempest-tossèd body. How now wife,
    Have you delivered to her our decree?

[139] will none   *will have none of it*

[140] I would . . . grave   *A line of dreadful irony. How does Lady Capulet behave when she thinks that Juliet really is dead?*

[141] Soft . . . you   *Wait a moment, I don't understand*

[143] count her   *consider herself*

[144] wrought   *persuaded*

[145] bride   *used for either sex in Shakespeare's time*

[146] Not . . . have   *I am not pleased that you have persuaded Paris to marry me but I am grateful*

[148] for . . . love   *something hateful to me when it is meant to show your love*

[149] chop-logic   *one who enjoys arguing*

[151] Mistress . . . you   *You saucy madame*

[152] Thank . . . thankings   *I don't want any of your 'thankings'*

[153] fettle   *set in order*
      'gainst   *ready for*

[155] hurdle   *Traitors were dragged to the place of execution on wooden hurdles. Capulet can be as savage as his wife when he is angry.*

[156] green-sickness carrion   *anaemic corpse*

[157] tallow-face   *pale-faced wretch*
      what . . . mad?   *Is she addressing Capulet or Juliet?*

LADY CAPULET Ay sir, but she will none, she gives
       you thanks.
      I would the fool were married to her grave.   140
CAPULET Soft, take me with you, take me with you,
       wife.
      How will she none? Doth she not give us
       thanks?
      Is she not proud? Doth she not count her
       blest,
      Unworthy as she is, that we have wrought
      So worthy a gentleman to be her bride?
JULIET Not proud you have, but thankful that you
       have.
      Proud can I never be of what I hate,
      But thankful even for hate that is meant love.
CAPULET How, how, how, how, chop-logic. What is
       this?
      'Proud', and, 'I thank you', and 'I thank you
       not',   150
      And yet 'not proud'? Mistress minion you,
      Thank me no thankings nor proud me no
       prouds,
      But fettle your fine joints 'gainst Thursday
       next,
      To go with Paris to Saint Peter's Church,
      Or I will drag thee on a hurdle thither.
      Out you green-sickness carrion, out you
       baggage,
      You tallow-face!
LADY CAPULET   Fie, fie! what, are you mad?
JULIET Good father, I beseech you on my knees,
      Hear me with patience, but to speak a word.
CAPULET Hang thee young baggage, disobedient
       wretch!   160
      I tell thee what, get thee to church a Thursday,
      Or never after look me in the face.
      Speak not, reply not, do not answer me.

[164] itch   *i.e. to hit her*

[164-7] Wife . . . her   *These are dreadful words – and full of irony.*

[168] hilding   *good-for-nothing creature*

[169] rate   *abuse*

[170-1] Wisdom . . . Prudence   *Capulet sinks to sarcasm.*

[171] Smatter . . . go   *Go and chatter with your gossiping friends*

[172] O . . . god-den   *Capulet's impatient way of telling her to go.*

[174] Utter . . . bowl   *Keep your weighty words for when you're drinking with your tattling friends*

[175] hot   *angry*

[176] God's bread   *a solemn oath by the bread consecrated in the Mass – singularly inappropriate from a cruel and angry man*

[177] tide   *season*

[178] still   *continually*

[179] matched   *married*

[181] demesnes   *estates*

nobly trained   *educated as befits a gentleman*

[182] Stuffed   *Packed full*

parts   *qualities*

[183] Proportioned   *Fashioned*

[184] puling   *whimpering*

[185] mammet . . . tender   *puppet, when fortune offers such a good chance (of marriage)*

[188] an   *if*

[189] Graze   *Capulet treats her like an animal – if she won't marry Paris, he won't provide food and a home for her.*

[190] do not use   *am not accustomed*

174

My fingers itch. Wife, we scarce thought us
    blest
That God had lent us but this only child;
But now I see this one is one too much,
And that we have a curse in having her.
Out on her, hilding!

NURSE   God in heaven bless her!
You are to blame, my lord, to rate her so.

CAPULET And why, my Lady Wisdom? Hold your
    tongue,   170
Good Prudence. Smatter with your gossips,
    go.

NURSE I speak no treason.

CAPULET   O God ye god-den.

NURSE May not one speak?

CAPULET   Peace, you mumbling fool.
Utter your gravity o'er a gossip's bowl,
For here we need it not.

LADY CAPULET   You are too hot.

CAPULET God's bread, it makes me mad.
Day, night, hour, tide, time, work, play,
Alone, in company, still my care hath been
To have her matched; and having now
    provided
A gentleman of noble parentage,   180
Of fair demesnes, youthful and nobly trained,
Stuffed, as they say, with honourable parts,
Proportioned as one's thought would wish a
    man –
And then to have a wretched puling fool,
A whining mammet, in her fortune's tender,
To answer 'I'll not wed, I cannot love,
I am too young, I pray you pardon me' –
But an you will not wed, I'll pardon you –
Graze where you will, you shall not house with
    me.
Look to't, think on't, I do not use to jest.   190

[191] lay . . . heart   *reflect*
      advise   *consider carefully*
[192] mine   *What does this tell us about Capulet's paternal love?*

[195] Nor . . . good   *And you shall never benefit from anything that belongs to me. Capulet falls back on threats when he is angry – compare I. 5. 85.*
[196] be forsworn   *go back on the threats I've just made and on my promise to Paris*

[201-2] Or if . . . lies   *Shakespeare continues to prepare the way for the ending of his play.*

[208-9] Unless . . . earth   *Juliet can be released from her marriage vows only if Romeo goes to heaven (dies).*
[209] Comfort me   *Juliet's repeated call for comfort and the Nurse's failure to respond provide one of the most poignant moments in the play.*
[210-11] practise . . . Upon   *contrive such violent plots against*
[211] soft a subject   *gentle a creature*

[214] all . . . nothing   *it's a million to one*
[215] challenge   *lay claim to*
[216] needs must be   *is bound to be*

[220] dishclout to him   *dishcloth compared to him*

Thursday is near, lay hand on heart, advise.
An you be mine, I'll give you to my friend;
An you be not, hang, beg, starve, die in the
    streets,
For by my soul, I'll ne'er acknowledge thee,
Nor what is mine shall never do thee good.
Trust to't; bethink you; I'll not be forsworn.

                                    [*Exit*

JULIET Is there no pity sitting in the clouds
That sees into the bottom of my grief?
O sweet my mother, cast me not away.
Delay this marriage for a month, a week,   200
Or if you do not, make the bridal bed
In that dim monument where Tybalt lies.

LADY CAPULET Talk not to me, for I'll not speak a
    word.
Do as thou wilt, for I have done with thee.

                                    [*Exit*

JULIET O God! O Nurse, how shall this be prevented?
My husband is on earth, my faith in heaven;
How shall that faith return again to earth,
Unless that husband send it me from heaven
By leaving earth? Comfort me, counsel me.
Alack, alack, that heaven should practise
    stratagems   210
Upon so soft a subject as myself!
What sayest thou? Hast thou not a word of joy?
Some comfort, nurse.

NURSE   Faith, here it is. Romeo
Is banishèd, and all the world to nothing,
That he dares ne'er come back to challenge
    you;
Or if he do, it needs must be by stealth.
Then since the case so stands as now it doth,
I think it best you married with the County.
O he's a lovely gentleman!
Romeo's a dishclout to him; an eagle, madam, 220

[221] **green**   *It seems that green eyes were greatly admired then.*
quick   *lively*

[222] **Beshrew**   *Cursed be*

[226] **As . . . him**   *As have him living here on earth with no profit to yourself*

[227] **Speak'st . . . heart?**   *Do you really mean that?*
soul   *One wonders what the Nurse's soul has to do with her suggestion that Juliet should commit bigamy.*

[228] **Amen**   *Juliet replies 'So be it' to the Nurse's 'Cursed be both my heart and soul' but the Nurse fails to understand to what 'Amen' refers.*

[229] **Well . . . much**   *A line packed with bitter ironic feeling.*

[230–2] **Go . . . absolved**   *Juliet shows her resourcefulness and is forced into further deceit by the harshness of her treatment.*

[234] **Ancient damnation**   *You old devil. The powerful conjunction of two heavy words of Latin origin enable the actress to put enormous bite into what she says.*

[235] **more sin**   *more wicked (of the Nurse)*
thus forsworn   *to be false to my marriage vows*

[237] **above**   *as being beyond*

[239] **Thou . . . twain**   *From now on I shall never take you into my trust*

[241] **If . . . die**   *The suicide note is again sounded.*

Hath not so green, so quick, so fair an eye
As Paris hath. Beshrew my very heart,
I think you are happy in this second match,
For it excels your first; or if it did not,
Your first is dead, or 'twere as good he were
As living here and you no use of him.

JULIET Speak'st thou from thy heart?

NURSE   And from my soul too.
Or else beshrew them both.

JULIET   Amen.

NURSE   What?

JULIET Well thou hast comforted me marvellous
    much.
Go in, and tell my lady I am gone,   230
Having displeased my father, to Lawrence'
    cell,
To make confession, and to be absolved.

NURSE Marry I will, and this is wisely done.   [Exit

JULIET Ancient damnation! O most wicked fiend!
Is it more sin to wish me thus forsworn,
Or to dispraise my lord with that same tongue
Which she hath praised him with above
    compare
So many thousand times? Go counsellor;
Thou and my bosom henceforth shall be twain.
I'll to the friar to know his remedy.   240
If all else fail, myself have power to die. [Exit

ACT FOUR, scene 1

Although it has been customary since the eighteenth century to divide Shakespeare's plays into acts and scenes, there is no real break here and the action moves uninterruptedly towards its climax in the tomb. We are now at Friar Lawrence's cell and Shakespeare has given the audience a clear hint at the end of the previous scene that this will be the location.

[1] The . . . short *The Friar knows that time is very important. We know that Paris has been discussing the wedding and can understand the Friar's alarm. Shakespeare works with great economy.*

[2] My father *There is something ironic in Paris's certainty about the future.*

[3] And . . . haste *And I shall in no way lessen his haste by being slow myself*

[5] Uneven . . . course *The procedure is irregular*

[8] Venus . . . tears *love and sorrow do not go well together*

[10] do . . . sway *gives way so much to her sorrow*

[13] too . . . alone *thought about too much when she is by herself*

[14] put . . . society *removed from her by having companionship*

[18–26] Happily . . . me *These lines illustrate the stylistic device, called stichomythia, where there occurs a series of one-line exchanges. It is more commonly found in Shakespeare's earlier plays.*

[20] must be *Is Shakespeare commenting on the nature of arranged marriages?*

[21] certain text *true saying*

ACT FOUR

Scene 1. *Enter* FRIAR LAWRENCE *and* PARIS

FRIAR LAWRENCE On Thursday sir? The time is very
    short.
PARIS My father Capulet will have it so,
    And I am nothing slow to slack his haste.
FRIAR LAWRENCE You say you do not know the lady's
    mind?
    Uneven is the course, I like it not.
PARIS Immoderately she weeps for Tybalt's death,
    And therefore have I little talked of love,
    For Venus smiles not in a house of tears.
    Now sir, her father counts it dangerous
    That she do give her sorrow so much sway,   10
    And in his wisdom hastes our marriage
    To stop the inundation of her tears,
    Which, too much minded by herself alone,
    May be put from her by society.
    Now do you know the reason of this haste.
FRIAR LAWRENCE [*Aside*] I would I knew not why it
    should be slowed.
    [*Aloud*] Look sir, here comes the lady toward
    my cell.

Enter JULIET

PARIS Happily met, my lady and my wife.
JULIET That may be sir, when I may be a wife.
PARIS That 'may be' must be, love, on Thursday
    next.   20
JULIET What must be shall be.
FRIAR LAWRENCE   That's a certain text.
PARIS Come you to make confession to this father?
JULIET To answer that, I should confess to you.
PARIS Do not deny to him that you love me.

181

[27] more price   *more valuable – what is said behind your back is more likely to be true than what is said to your face*

[29] abused   *disfigured*

[31] spite   *injury*

[34] to my face   *openly, about my face*

[36] it . . . own   *because it has been given to Romeo*

[39] My . . . me   *I am free*
     pensive   *sorrowful*
[40] entreat . . . alone   *beg you to leave us alone now*
[41] shield   *forbid that*

[43] holy kiss   *Is there irony in the use of 'holy' in this context?*

[47] compass . . . wits   *limits of my mental powers*
[48] prorogue   *postpone*

[53] resolution   *decision, i.e. as she explains in the next line, the decision to commit suicide*
[54] presently   *at once*

[56] sealed   *joined – this leads on to the idea of the wax seal on a legal document*

JULIET I will confess to you that I love him.

PARIS So will ye, I am sure, that you love me.

JULIET If I do so, it will be of more price,
    Being spoke behind your back, than to your
      face.

PARIS Poor soul, thy face is much abused with tears.

JULIET The tears have got small victory by that,   30
    For it was bad enough before their spite.

PARIS Thou wrong'st it more than tears with that
    report.

JULIET That is no slander sir, which is a truth,
    And what I spake, I spake it to my face.

PARIS Thy face is mine, and thou hast slandered it.

JULIET It may be so, for it is not mine own.
    Are you at leisure, holy father, now,
    Or shall I come to you at evening mass?

FRIAR LAWRENCE My leisure serves me, pensive
    daughter, now.
    My lord, we must entreat the time alone.   40

PARIS God shield I should disturb devotion!
    Juliet, on Thursday early will I rouse ye.
    Till then adieu, and keep this holy kiss. [*Exit*

JULIET O shut the door, and when thou hast done so,
    Come weep with me, past hope, past cure,
      past help.

FRIAR LAWRENCE O Juliet I already know thy grief,
    It strains me past the compass of my wits.
    I hear thou must, and nothing may prorogue it,
    On Thursday next be married to this County.

JULIET Tell me not friar, that thou hear'st of this,   50
    Unless thou tell me how I may prevent it.
    If in thy wisdom thou canst give no help,
    Do thou but call my resolution wise
    And with this knife I'll help it presently.
    God joined my heart and Romeo's, thou our
      hands;
    And ere this hand, by thee to Romeo's sealed,

[57] label   *the slip of paper or parchment for joining a seal to a document*

deed   *legal document – but Juliet means 'marriage contract'*

[59] this   *the knife*

both   *i.e. hand and heart*

[60] out . . . time   *life of long experience*

[61] present counsel   *immediate advice*

[62–5] 'Twixt . . . bring   *This bloody knife shall judge between me and my miseries, and will settle that which not even you with all the authority of your age and skill could bring to a truly honourable conclusion*

[66] Be . . . speak   *Do say something quickly*

[67] If . . . remedy   *If what you have to say does not speak to me of some way out of my troubles*

[68] Hold   *Wait*

[69] craves . . . execution   *demands as much desperation in putting it into effect*

[74] chide   *drive*

[75] That . . . it   *(you) who are willing to meet death itself in order to escape the shame of marrying Paris*

[79] in thievish ways   *places where thieves are found*

[81] nightly   *at night*

charnel-house   *a small building in a church-yard where bones were deposited when they were unearthed in the digging of new graves*

[81–5] Or . . . shroud   *Juliet unwittingly describes her fate in V. 3.*

[82] O'er-covered quite   *Completely covered with*

[83] reeky shanks   *stinking shin-bones*

chapless   *without lower jaws*

Shall be the label to another deed,
Or my true heart with treacherous revolt
Turn to another, this shall slay them both.
Therefore, out of thy long-experienced time,   60
Give me some present counsel, or, behold,
'Twixt my extremes and me this bloody knife
Shall play the umpire, arbitrating that
Which the commission of thy years and art
Could to no issue of true honour bring.
Be not so long to speak; I long to die
If what thou speak'st speak not of remedy.

FRIAR LAWRENCE Hold daughter, I do spy a kind of
          hope,
Which craves as desperate an execution
As that is desperate which we would prevent.   70
If, rather than to marry County Paris,
Thou hast the strength of will to slay thyself,
Then is it likely thou wilt undertake
A thing like death to chide away this shame,
That cop'st with death himself to 'scape from
          it;
And if thou darest, I'll give thee remedy.

JULIET O bid me leap, rather than marry Paris,
From off the battlements of any tower;
Or walk in thievish ways; or bid me lurk
Where serpents are; chain me with roaring
          bears;   80
Or hide me nightly in a charnel-house,
O'er-covered quite with dead men's rattling
          bones,
With reeky shanks and yellow chapless skulls;
Or bid me go into a new-made grave,
And hide me with a dead man in his shroud –
Things that to hear them told have made me
          tremble –
And I will do it without fear or doubt,
To live an unstained wife to my sweet love.

[91] look ... alone *make sure that you sleep alone*

[93] vial *phial, bottle*

[94] distillèd *i.e. obtained by distillation – we remember the Friar's knowledge of drugs (II. 3)*

[95] presently *at once*

[96] humour *fluid*

[97] native progress *natural movement*
  surcease *cease*

[100] wanny *pale*
  eyes' windows *eyes' shutters, i.e. eyelids*

[102] supple government *the power of movement*

[104] borrowed *false*

[105] two ... hours *Juliet takes the drug on Tuesday night and wakes up in the tomb on Thursday night. The timing is important as Shakespeare makes clear.*

[107] the bridegroom *i.e. Paris*

[110] uncovered *with face uncovered*

[113] against *in readiness for the time*

[114] drift *plan*

[119] inconstant toy *irresolute fancy*

[120] Abate *Weaken*
  the ... it *carrying it out*

FRIAR LAWRENCE Hold then, go home, be merry, give
        consent
        To marry Paris. Wednesday is tomorrow;   90
        Tomorrow night look that thou lie alone,
        Let not the nurse lie with thee in thy chamber.
        Take thou this vial, being then in bed,
        And this distillèd liquor drink thou off,
        When presently through all thy veins shall run
        A cold and drowsy humour; for no pulse
        Shall keep his native progress, but surcease;
        No warmth, no breath, shall testify thou livest;
        The roses in thy lips and cheeks shall fade
        To wanny ashes; thy eyes' windows fall,   100
        Like death when he shuts up the day of life.
        Each part, deprived of supple government,
        Shall stiff and stark and cold appear like death,
        And in this borrowed likeness of shrunk
            death
        Thou shalt continue two and forty hours,
        And then awake as from a pleasant sleep.
        Now when the bridegroom in the morning
            comes
        To rouse thee from thy bed, there art thou
            dead.
        Then, as the manner of our country is,
        In thy best robes uncovered on the bier,   110
        Thou shalt be borne to that same ancient vault,
        Where all the kindred of the Capulets lie.
        In the meantime, against thou shalt awake,
        Shall Romeo by my letters know our drift,
        And hither shall he come; and he and I
        Will watch thy waking, and that very night
        Shall Romeo bear thee hence to Mantua.
        And this shall free thee from this present
            shame,
        If no inconstant toy nor womanish fear
        Abate thy valour in the acting it.   120

[121] Give me   *i.e. the bottle*
[122] prosperous   *successful*

[125] help afford   *provide help*

ACT FOUR, scene 2

Capulet's preparations for the wedding remind the audience of his feast (I. 5) which, because of the sheer density of the action now seems in the distant past even though we are aware at the same time that it was only two days ago. Ironically, Juliet's deceit causes her father to advance the wedding day from Thursday to Wednesday, and haste and impulsiveness again play a part in causing the fatal end of the play.

[2] cunning   *skilful*
[3] none ill   *no bad cooks*
[4] can . . . fingers   *i.e. taste his food. It would be a sign of a bad cook if he didn't want to taste his food.*
[8] goes not with me   *is not acceptable to me*
[10] We . . . time   *We shall not have everything ready in time*
[12] forsooth   *in truth, certainly*

[14] A . . . is   *She is an obstinate, headstrong, silly girl*
[15] shrift   *confession*

[16] gadding   *wandering*

188

JULIET Give me, give me. O tell not me of fear.
FRIAR LAWRENCE Hold. Get you gone, be strong and
    prosperous
    In this resolve. I'll send a friar with speed
    To Mantua with my letters to thy lord.
JULIET Love give me strength, and strength shall help
    afford.
    Farewell dear father.

                                            [Exeunt

Scene 2. *Enter* CAPULET, LADY CAPULET, NURSE *and*
SERVINGMEN

CAPULET So many guests invite as here are writ.
                             [Exit FIRST SERVANT
    Sirrah, go hire me twenty cunning cooks.
SECOND SERVANT You shall have none ill sir, for I'll
    try if they can lick their fingers.
CAPULET How canst thou try them so?
SECOND SERVANT Marry sir, 'tis an ill cook that cannot
    lick his own fingers; therefore he that cannot lick his
    fingers goes not with me.
CAPULET Go, be gone.
                               [Exit SERVANT
    We shall be much unfurnished for this time.   10
    What, is my daughter gone to Friar Lawrence?
NURSE Ay forsooth.
CAPULET Well, he may chance to do some good on
    her;
    A peevish self-willed harlotry it is.
NURSE See where she comes from shrift with merry
    look.

Enter JULIET

CAPULET How now my headstrong, where have you
    been gadding?

[19] behests   *commands*
  enjoined   *directed (as part of my penance)*

[22] I am ever   *I will always be*

[24] knot . . . up   *marriage solemnized*
  tomorrow morning   *i.e. Wednesday which he had previously said was too soon (III. 4. 19). Juliet's exaggerated repentance has disastrous consequences.*

[26] becomèd   *befitting*

[29] Let . . . County   *This is sometimes punctuated as if Capulet has forgotten what he intended to say, but this seems out of character, and the sense 'Arrange for me to see Paris' fits in well.*

[32] bound to him   *in his debt – more irony*

[33] closet   *own room*

[34] sort . . . ornaments   *choose such necessary clothes and jewellery*

[35] to furnish me   *for me to wear*

[38] We . . . provision   *We shall not have ready everything we need to provide*

[40] warrant   *assure*

[41] deck   *dress*

[42] Let me alone   *Leave it to me*

[44] They . . . forth   *The cry 'What ho!' has produced no reply from the servants, so Capulet says, 'They are all gone.'*

[46] Against   *Ready for*

[47] is so reclaimed   *has been brought back to obedience*

JULIET Where I have learned me to repent the sin
       Of disobedient opposition
       To you and your behests, and am enjoined
       By holy Lawrence to fall prostrate here,   20
       To beg your pardon. Pardon I beseech you;
       Henceforward I am ever ruled by you.

CAPULET Send for the County, go tell him of this.
        I'll have this knot knit up tomorrow morning.

JULIET I met the youthful lord at Lawrence cell,
       And gave him what becomèd love I might,
       Not stepping o'er the bounds of modesty.

CAPULET Why I am glad on 't; this is well. Stand up.
        This is as 't should be. Let me see the County.
        Ay, marry, go, I say, and fetch him hither.   30
        Now afore God, this reverend holy friar,
        All our whole city is much bound to him.

JULIET Nurse, will you go with me into my closet
       To help me sort such needful ornaments
       As you think fit to furnish me tomorrow?

LADY CAPULET No, not till Thursday, there is time
             enough.

CAPULET Go nurse, go with her; we'll to church
        tomorrow.

                              [Exeunt JULIET and NURSE

LADY CAPULET We shall be short in our provision;
             'Tis now near night.

CAPULET   Tush, I will stir about,
        And all things shall be well, I warrant thee,
             wife.   40
        Go thou to Juliet, help to deck up her;
        I'll not to bed tonight. Let me alone.
        I'll play the housewife for this once. What ho!
        They are all forth. Well, I will walk myself
        To County Paris, to prepare up him
        Against tomorrow. My heart is wondrous light
        Since this same wayward girl is so reclaimed.

                                             [Exeunt

ROMEO AND JULIET

ACT FOUR, scene 3

Juliet has talked about going to her room and we move quickly to it. She is forced to take the drug a day earlier because Capulet has brought the wedding-day forward to Wednesday. Her soliloquy is regarded by some as a magnificent piece of moving poetry, and by others as an unnecessary display of melodramatic virtuosity by an immature Shakespeare.

[1] attires   *clothes*
   gentle Nurse   *Juliet is playing a game. We know what she really thinks about the Nurse.*
[3] orisons   *prayers*
[5] cross   *quarrelsome*
[7] culled   *picked out*
[8] behoveful   *necessary*
   state   *i.e. of being married*

[15] faint cold fear   *fear causing faintness and cold*
   thrills   *shivers*

[17] comfort me   *She may remember what happened when she last asked the Nurse for comfort. She is desperately alone.*
[19] dismal   *horrible*

[23] this   *this dagger*

Scene 3. *Enter* JULIET *and* NURSE

JULIET   Ay, those attires are best; but gentle Nurse,
        I pray thee leave me to myself tonight;
        For I have need of many orisons
        To move the heavens to smile upon my state,
        Which well thou knowest is cross and full of
          sin.

Enter LADY CAPULET

LADY CAPULET What, are you busy, ho? Need you my
        help?
JULIET No madam, we have culled such necessaries
        As are behoveful for our state tomorrow.
        So please you, let me now be left alone,
        And let the Nurse this night sit up with you,   10
        For I am sure you have your hands full all
        In this so sudden business.
LADY CAPULET   Good night.
        Get thee to bed and rest, for thou hast need.
          [*Exeunt* LADY CAPULET *and* NURSE
JULIET Farewell. God knows when we shall meet
        again.
        I have a faint cold fear thrills through my
        veins,
        That almost freezes up the heat of life.
        I'll call them back again to comfort me.
        Nurse! What should she do here?
        My dismal scene I needs must act alone.
        Come vial.   20
        What if this mixture do not work at all?
        Shall I be married then tomorrow morning?
        No, no, this shall forbid it. Lie thou there.

Lays down a dagger

        What if it be a poison which the friar

[25] Subtly . . . ministered *Cunningly has provided*

[29] hath . . . tried *has always been proved to be*

[32] redeem *rescue*

[34] healthsome *healthy*

[35] strangled *suffocated*
[36] like *likely*
[37] conceit . . . night *fancies produced by thoughts of death and night*

[39] receptacle *sepulchre*

[42] green *fresh*
[43] festering *rotting*

[46] So early waking *i.e. Before Romeo arrives*
[47] mandrakes' *The mandrake or mandragora was a plant famous for its medicinal qualities. When pulled from the earth it was believed to utter a shriek which would drive hearers mad.*
[48] That *So that*
[49] distraught *mad*

[53] rage *madness*
   great kinsman's *such as a great-grandfather*

[56] spit *pierce*

Subtly hath ministered to have me dead,
Lest in this marriage he should be dishonoured,
Because he married me before to Romeo?
I fear it is, and yet methinks it should not,
For he hath still been tried a holy man.
How if, when I am laid into the tomb,   30
I wake before the time that Romeo
Come to redeem me? There's a fearful point.
Shall I not then be stifled in the vault,
To whose foul mouth no healthsome air
    breathes in,
And there die strangled ere my Romeo comes?
Or if I live, is it not very like,
The horrible conceit of death and night,
Together with the terror of the place –
As in a vault, an ancient receptacle,
Where for this many hundred years the bones   40
Of all my buried ancestors are packed,
Where bloody Tybalt yet but green in earth
Lies festering in his shroud, where as they
    say,
At some hours in the night spirits resort –
Alack, alack, is it not like that I,
So early waking – what with loathsome smells,
And shrieks like mandrakes' torn out of the
    earth,
That living mortals hearing them, run mad –
O if I wake, shall I not be distraught,
Environèd with all these hideous fears,   50
And madly play with my forefathers' joints,
And pluck the mangled Tybalt from his
    shroud,
And in this rage, with some great kinsman's
    bone,
As with a club, dash out my desperate brains?
O look, methinks I see my cousin's ghost
Seeking out Romeo that did spit his body

[57] stay *stop. She imagines that Tybalt is attacking Romeo. Tybalt, though dead, remains an important symbol of hate and violence.*

the curtains *The part of the acting area at the rear of the main stage provided a useful room which could be closed off with curtains. Juliet's bed is here and the curtains are pulled to for the next scene and then drawn to reveal the apparently dead Juliet in scene 5.*

ACT FOUR, scene 4

A lull before the storm. This comic interlude in which preparations are made for a wedding which will never take place is full of irony and provides the necessary lapse of time between Juliet's taking the drug and her discovery by the Nurse.

[1] spices *Spices were valuable and were kept locked away.*

[2] pastry *pastryroom*

[4] curfew *The bell was rung not only in the evening but at three or four o'clock in the morning.*

[5] baked meats *meat pies and other pastries*

Angelica *probably the name of the Nurse although it is not clear that Capulet is addressing her*

[6] Spare . . . cost *Don't worry about the expense*

cot-quean *name given to a man who meddles with women's domestic work*

[8] watching *keeping awake*

[9] whit *bit*

[11] mouse-hunt *woman-chaser*

[12] watch *prevent*

[13] jealous hood *jealous woman – but it might be 'jealous-hood' meaning 'jealousy'*

Upon a rapier's point – stay Tybalt, stay!
Romeo, I come! this do I drink to thee.

She falls upon her bed within the curtains

Scene 4. *Enter* LADY CAPULET *and* NURSE

LADY CAPULET Hold, take these keys, and fetch more
        spices, Nurse.
NURSE They call for dates and quinces in the pastry.

Enter old CAPULET

CAPULET Come, stir, stir, stir, the second cock hath
        crowed,
        The curfew bell hath rung, 'tis three o'clock.
        Look to the baked meats, good Angelica.
        Spare not for cost.
NURSE   Go you cot-quean, go,
        Get you to bed; faith you'll be sick tomorrow
        For this night's watching.
CAPULET No, not a whit; what, I have watched ere
        now
        All night for lesser cause, and ne'er been sick.   10
LADY CAPULET Ay you have been a mouse-hunt in
        your time,
        But I will watch you from such watching
        now.
            [*Exeunt* LADY CAPULET *and* NURSE
CAPULET A jealous hood, a jealous hood!

Enter three or four SERVINGMEN, *with spits, and logs,
and baskets*

                        Now fellow,
What is there?

[20] whoreson *fellow*

[21] Thou . . . logger-head *We shall call you blockhead*

[22] with music *It was a custom to wake the bride on her wedding day with music.*

straight *straightway*

[25] trim her up *dress her*

[27] the . . . already *Ironically, Juliet's bridegroom has come already, but Capulet does not know it.*

ACT FOUR, scene 5

The Nurse stays on the stage, pulls the curtains of the inner stage, and reveals Juliet on the bed. The scene of lamentation which follows is difficult to interpret. Some have seen it as crudely written, others as a valuable comment on the characters of the mourners. With the farce of Peter and the musicians rounding it off, it is possible to regard this as a last piece of comedy before tragedy takes over completely. Shakespeare can mock the mourners because they mourn someone who is alive and they show more feeling towards Juliet supposedly dead than Juliet alive. The Nurse would be out of place in Act V and we see no more of her.

[1] Fast *i.e. fast asleep*

[2] slug-a-bed *lazy person*

[4] You . . . now *You make sure that you get your money's worth of sleep now*

FIRST SERVINGMAN Things for the cook sir, but I
    know not what.
CAPULET Make haste, make haste. Sirrah, fetch drier
    logs.
    Call Peter, he will show thee where they are.
SECOND SERVINGMAN I have a head sir, that will find
    out logs,
    And never trouble Peter for the matter. [*Exit*
CAPULET Mass, and well said; a merry whoreson, ha!   20
    Thou shalt be logger-head. Good faith, 'tis
    day.
    The County will be here with music straight,

              Music within

    For so he said he would. I hear him near.
    Nurse! Wife! What ho! What, Nurse I say!

              Enter NURSE

    Go waken Juliet, go and trim her up.
    I'll go and chat with Paris. Hie, make haste,
    Make haste; the bridegroom he is come
    already.
    Make haste I say.

                     [*Exeunt*

Scene 5. *Enter* NURSE

NURSE Mistress! What, mistress! Juliet! Fast, I
    warrant her. She –
    Why lamb, why lady – fie you slug-a-bed!
    Why love I say! Madam! Sweet-heart! Why
    bride!
    What, not a word? You take your pennyworths
    now.

[6] set . . . rest *staked everything – with a bawdy pun. The Nurse is unchangeable. There was the same lewdness when Romeo came as bridegroom.*

[7] God . . . me! *The Nurse's religious exclamations are almost meaningless.*

[11] Will. . . be? *Will you not wake up?*

[12] down again *lain down again*

[15] weraday *well-a-day, alas*
[16] aqua vitae *brandy or other strong spirits*

[19] me . . . me . . . my . . . my *The emphasis on self is significant.*
[26] is settled *has come to rest*

Sleep for a week; for the next night I warrant
The County Paris hath set up his rest
That you shall rest but little. God forgive me!
Marry, and amen. How sound is she asleep!
I needs must wake her. Madam, madam, madam!
Ay, let the County take you in your bed,   10
He'll fright you up i' faith. Will it not be?

Draws back the curtains

What, dressed, and in your clothes, and down again?
I must needs wake you. Lady, lady, lady!
Alas, alas, help, help, my lady's dead!
O weraday that ever I was born!
Some aqua vitae ho! My lord! My lady!

Enter LADY CAPULET

LADY CAPULET What noise is here?
NURSE   O lamentable day!
LADY CAPULET What is the matter?
NURSE   Look, look. O heavy day!
LADY CAPULET O me, O me, my child, my only life!
Revive, look up, or I will die with thee.   20
Help, help! Call help.

Enter CAPULET

CAPULET For shame, bring Juliet forth; her lord is
come.
NURSE She's dead, deceased, she's dead, alack the
day!
LADY CAPULET Alack the day, she's dead, she's dead,
she's dead!
CAPULET Ha! Let me see her. Out alas! she's cold,
Her blood is settled, and her joints are stiff;

[28] untimely   *come at the wrong time, out of season*

Musicians   *Granville-Barker thinks it likely that the musicians 'stay playing the bridal music without, a tragical ironical accompaniment to the lamenting over Juliet, till they are stopped and come clustering into the doorway'. The First Quarto puts the entry of the Musicians after line 95.*

[36] Hath . . . wife   *More imagery on the theme of death as Juliet's lover.*

[38] Death . . . heir   *The emphasis on having descendants to inherit his wealth reappears in line 40. Hatred has led to death which inherits all.*

[40] living   *means of living, i.e. property and money*

[41] thought long   *He may have been thinking of the possibility of marrying Juliet for a long time.*

[45] lasting . . . pilgrimage   *in the never-ending work of his (Time's) journey from era to era*

[46] But one   *Shakespeare wants us to remember that Juliet is an only child.*

[47] solace in   *find comfort in*

[48] catched   *snatched*

[49–54] O woe . . . day!   *It is difficult not to believe that Shakespeare meant his audience to laugh at this ridiculous outburst, particularly as it echoes the exaggerated language found in Pyramus's comic speech in* A Midsummer Night's Dream *– beginning 'O grim-looked night! O night with hue so black!' – which would have been being performed about the same time as* Romeo and Juliet.

Life and these lips have long been separated.
Death lies on her like an untimely frost
Upon the sweetest flower of all the field.
NURSE O lamentable day!
LADY CAPULET   O woeful time!   30
CAPULET Death that hath ta'en her hence to make me
    wail,
    Ties up my tongue, and will not let me speak.

Enter FRIAR LAWRENCE, PARIS *and*
    MUSICIANS

FRIAR LAWRENCE Come, is the bride ready to go to
    church?
CAPULET Ready to go, but never to return.
    O son, the night before thy wedding-day
    Hath Death lain with thy wife; there she lies,
    Flower as she was, deflowerèd by him.
    Death is my son-in-law, Death is my heir,
    My daughter he hath wedded. I will die
    And leave him all; life, living, all is Death's.   40
PARIS Have I thought long to see this morning's face,
    And doth it give me such a sight as this?
LADY CAPULET Accursed, unhappy, wretched, hateful
    day!
    Most miserable hour that e'er Time saw
    In lasting labour of his pilgrimage!
    But one, poor one, one poor and loving child,
    But one thing to rejoice and solace in,
    And cruel Death hath catched it from my
    sight.
NURSE O woe! O woeful, woeful, woeful day!
    Most lamentable day, most woeful day   50
    That ever, ever, I did yet behold!
    O day! O day! O day! O hateful day!
    Never was seen so black a day as this.
    O woeful day! O woeful day!

[55] Beguiled   *Cheated*
　　 divorcèd   *separated*
　　 spited   *injured. Paris is referring to himself. Why does Shakespeare stress the self-pity of the mourners?*

[58] Not . . . death!   *No longer my life but still my love though dead*

[60] Uncomfortable   *Distressing*
[61] solemnity   *festivity*

[65–6] Confusion's . . . confusions   *The putting right of this fatal blow doesn't lie in these noisy outbursts*

[67] Had part   *Had a share*

[69] Your part   *i.e. her physical self*
[70] his part   *i.e. her soul*
[71] promotion   *advancement – through marriage*
[72] 'twas . . . advanced   *it was your greatest happiness that she should be raised in status by marriage*
[75–6] O . . . well   *O, in this selfish earthly love there is really so little genuine love that you become desperate although Juliet has gone to heaven and all is well with her*
[77–8] She's . . . young   *The Friar says that it is good to die young – a good text but not easily acceptable by mere mortals.*
[79] rosemary   *an evergreen shrub regarded as a symbol of remembrance. It was used at both funerals and weddings.*
[80] corse   *corpse*
[81] In . . . church   *Why does the Friar go into such detail?*
[82] fond   *weak, affectionate*
　　 nature   *natural feeling*
[83] Yet . . . merriment   *yet reason laughs at our natural grief – because the dead have gone to a far happier place and we should rejoice rather than cry*
[84–5] All things . . . funeral   *All things designed for the marriage festivity must change from their allotted use to that of a mournful funeral*
[86] instruments   *musical instruments*
[87] cheer   *banquet*

PARIS Beguiled, divorcèd, wrongèd, spited, slain,
Most detestable Death, by thee beguiled,
By cruel, cruel thee quite overthrown.
O love! O life! Not life, but love in death!

CAPULET Despised, distressèd, hated, martyred, killed;
Uncomfortable time, why cam'st thou now 60
To murder, murder our solemnity?
O child! O child! My soul and not my child!
Dead art thou, alack my child is dead,
And with my child my joys are burièd.

FRIAR LAWRENCE Peace ho, for shame! Confusion's cure lives not
In these confusions. Heaven and yourself
Had part in this fair maid; now heaven hath all,
And all the better is it for the maid.
Your part in her you could not keep from death,
But heaven keeps his part in eternal life. 70
The most you sought was her promotion,
For 'twas your heaven she should be advanced;
And weep ye now, seeing she is advanced
Above the clouds, as high as heaven itself?
O in this love you love your child so ill,
That you run mad, seeing that she is well.
She's not well married that lives married long,
But she's best married that dies married young.
Dry up your tears, and stick your rosemary
On this fair corse; and as the custom is, 80
In all her best array bear her to church;
For though fond nature bids us all lament,
Yet nature's tears are reason's merriment.

CAPULET All things that we ordainèd festival
Turn from their office to black funeral:
Our instruments to melancholy bells;
Our wedding cheer to a sad burial feast;

[88] solemn hymns *festive songs*
    sullen dirges *mournful funeral songs*
[90] contrary *opposite*

[94] lour *frown*
    for some ill *because of some sin. There is more irony in this than the Friar realises.*
[95] Move . . . crossing *Anger the heavens no more by opposing*

[96] put up *pack up*
    pipes *musical instruments*
[98] pitiful case *sad state of affairs – but there is some punning on sexual meanings here and elsewhere in this interlude of the musicians.*
[99] amended *repaired. He confuses the Nurse's 'case' with his instrument case.*
Enter Peter *The Second Quarto has 'Enter Will Kemp'. Kemp was the leading comic actor in Shakespeare's company and presumably played the part of Peter.*

[100] 'Heart's ease' *a popular song of the time*

[101] and *if*

[103-4] 'My . . . full' *probably another popular song*
[104] dump *song*

[106] Not . . . we *We won't play a song*

[110] give . . . soundly *pay you out thoroughly*

[112] gleek *jest*
[112-13] I . . . minstrel *I'll call you 'minstrels' – a contemptuous term*

Our solemn hymns to sullen dirges change;
Our bridal flowers serve for a buried corse;
And all things change them to the contrary.   90
FRIAR LAWRENCE Sir, go you in, and madam, go with
    him;
    And go Sir Paris; every one prepare
    To follow this fair corse unto her grave.
    The heavens do lour upon you for some ill;
    Move them no more by crossing their high will.

They all but the NURSE *and* MUSICIANS *go forth, casting
rosemary on her and shutting the curtains*

FIRST MUSICIAN Faith we may put up our pipes and be
    gone.
NURSE Honest good fellows, ah put up, put up,
    For well you know this is a pitiful case. [*Exit*
FIRST MUSICIAN Ay by my troth, the case may be
    amended.

Enter PETER

PETER Musicians, O musicians, 'Heart's ease', 'Heart's
    ease'.   100
    O and you will have me live, play 'Heart's
    ease'.
FIRST MUSICIAN Why 'Heart's ease'?
PETER O musicians, because my heart itself plays 'My
    heart is full'. O play me some merry dump to
    comfort me.
FIRST MUSICIAN Not a dump we! 'Tis no time to
    play now.
PETER You will not then?
FIRST MUSICIAN No.
PETER I will then give it you soundly.   110
FIRST MUSICIAN What will you give us?
PETER No money on my faith, but the gleek. I will
    give you the minstrel.

[114–15] Will . . . serving-creature *I'll call you the serving-creature – another contemptuous term*

[117] pate *head*

I . . . crotchets *I won't put up with any of your silly ideas (musical notes)*

I'll . . . you *I'll give you music – possibly with a pun on 'ray' meaning 'to make dirty' and 'far' meaning to 'remove to a great distance'. 'Re' and 'fa' are the second and fourth notes on the musical scale.*

[118] Do . . . me? *Do you note what I say? There is a pun on a musical 'note', and 'do' and 'me' are the first and third notes on the musical scale.*

[119] An . . . us *If you set us to music*

[121] put out *extinguish, display. The Musician may mean the former and Peter understand the latter.*

[122] have . . . you *I shall attack you*

[123] put up *put away*

iron *merciless*

[125] griping *agonising*

[126] dumps *sorrows*

[129] Catling *the name of a catgut lute string. The Musicians have appropriate names.*

[130] silver . . . sound *the sound of money is attractive*

[132] Pretty *A neat answer*

Rebeck *a violin*

[134] sound for silver *play for money*

[135] Soundpost *part of a violin*

[137] cry you mercy *beg pardon*

[139] sounding *playing, jingling in their purses*

[141] lend redress *bring compensation*

[142] pestilent knave *scurvy rascal*

[143] Jack *ill-mannered fellow*

[144] stay *wait for*

FIRST MUSICIAN Then will I give you the serving-creature.

PETER Then will I lay the serving-creature's dagger on your pate. I will carry no crotchets. I'll *re* you, I'll *fa* you. Do you note me?

FIRST MUSICIAN An you *re* us and *fa* us, you note us.

SECOND MUSICIAN Pray you put up your dagger, 120 and put out your wit.

PETER Then have at you with my wit. I will dry-beat you with an iron wit, and put up my iron dagger. Answer me like men.

    'When griping grief the heart doth wound,
      And doleful dumps the mind oppress,
      Then music with her silver sound' –

Why 'silver sound'? Why 'music with her silver sound'? What say you Simon Catling?

FIRST MUSICIAN Marry sir, because silver hath a sweet 130 sound.

PETER Pretty. What say you Hugh Rebeck?

SECOND MUSICIAN I say 'silver sound', because musicians sound for silver.

PETER Pretty too. What say you James Soundpost?

THIRD MUSICIAN Faith I know not what to say.

PETER O I cry you mercy; you are the singer. I will say for you. It is 'music with her silver sound', because musicians have no gold for sounding.

    'Then music with her silver sound, 140
      With speedy help doth lend redress.' [*Exit*

FIRST MUSICIAN What a pestilent knave is this same!

SECOND MUSICIAN Hang him, Jack! Come we'll in here, tarry for the mourners, and stay dinner.

                [*Exeunt*

ACT FIVE, scene 1

Shakespeare frequently allowed his chief actors a period of rest before they had to face the demands of the closing scenes. Romeo has been off stage throughout Act IV and his entrance now tells the audience that the scene is probably Mantua. The poignancy is increased by letting Romeo have hopes of good news which are destroyed almost immediately. Ironically his love for Juliet and his impulsiveness drive him to immediate action in spite of Balthasar's advice to be patient.

[1] flattering   *illusory*

[2] presage   *foretell*

[3] bosom's lord   *love*
     lightly   *cheerfully*
     throne   *heart*

[6] I dreamt . . . dead   *another unwitting forecast of coming events*

[10] love . . . possessed   *the enjoying of love itself*

[11] but . . . shadows   *the mere dreams of love*
booted   *He has been riding.*

[12] Balthasar   *accent on the third syllable*

[18] monument   *burial vault. Balthasar has arrived before the Friar's letter.*

[21] presently . . . post   *I immediately started my journey using post-horses*

[23] Since . . . office   *Since you left me with the duty of bringing you any news*

[24] I . . . stars   *Romeo, the star-crossed lover, challenges the stars who have caused him so much misfortune.*

ACT FIVE

Scene 1. *Enter* ROMEO

ROMEO If I may trust the flattering truth of sleep,
    My dreams presage some joyful news at hand.
    My bosom's lord sits lightly in his throne,
    And all this day an unaccustomed spirit
    Lifts me above the ground with cheerful
      thoughts.
    I dreamt my lady came and found me dead –
    Strange dream that gives a dead man leave to
      think –
    And breathed such life with kisses in my lips
    That I revived, and was an emperor.
    Ah me, how sweet is love itself possessed,   10
    When but love's shadows are so rich in joy.

Enter BALTHASAR *his man, booted*

    News from Verona. How now Balthasar,
    Dost thou not bring me letters from the friar?
    How doth my lady? Is my father well?
    How fares my Juliet? That I ask again,
    For nothing can be ill if she be well.
BALTHASAR Then she is well and nothing can be ill.
    Her body sleeps in Capels' monument,
    And her immortal part with angels lives.
    I saw her laid low in her kindred's vault,   20
    And presently took post to tell it you.
    O pardon me for bringing these ill news,
    Since you did leave it for my office sir.
ROMEO Is it e'en so? Then I defy you, stars.
    Thou knowest my lodging, get me ink and
      paper,
    And hire post-horses; I will hence tonight.
BALTHASAR I do beseech you sir, have patience.

[28–9] import . . . misadventure *imply that some misfortune will happen*

[33] straight *immediately*

[34] lie with *embrace, sleep with. In one sense he will become Juliet's lover – in death.*

[35] for means *how I can arrange it*

mischief *evil*

[37] apothecary *a seller of drugs and medicines*

[38] 'a *he*

late I noted *I recently noticed*

[39] weeds *clothes*

overwhelming brows *large overhanging eyebrows*

[40] Culling of simples *Choosing medicinal herbs*

meagre . . . looks *he looked thin*

[42] needy *poor*

[45] beggarly account *miserable collection*

[46] earthen *earthenware*

bladders *receptacles for storing liquid*

[47] packthread *a strong thread used for sewing packs*

cakes of roses *cakes of compressed rose-petals used for perfume*

[48] to . . . show *to impress customers*

[49] penury *poverty*

[50] 'An if *If*

[51] is . . . death *is punished by immediate death*

[52] caitiff *miserable*

[53] forerun *anticipate*

Your looks are pale and wild, and do import
Some misadventure.

ROMEO   Tush, thou art deceived.
Leave me, and do the thing I bid thee do.   30
Hast thou no letters to me from the friar?

BALTHASAR No my good lord.

ROMEO   No matter. Get thee gone,
And hire those horses; I'll be with thee
    straight.

                              [*Exit* BALTHASAR

Well, Juliet, I will lie with thee tonight.
Let's see for means. O mischief thou art
    swift
To enter in the thoughts of desperate men.
I do remember an apothecary –
And hereabouts 'a dwells – which late I
    noted,
In tattered weeds, with overwhelming brows,
Culling of simples; meagre were his looks;   40
Sharp misery had worn him to the bones;
And in his needy shop a tortoise hung,
An alligator stuffed, and other skins
Of ill-shaped fishes, and about his shelves
A beggarly account of empty boxes,
Green earthen pots, bladders, and musty seeds,
Remnants of packthread, and old cakes of
    roses
Were thinly scattered, to make up a show.
Noting this penury, to myself I said,
'An if a man did need a poison now,   50
Whose sale is present death in Mantua,
Here lives a caitiff wretch would sell it him.'
O this same thought did but forerun my need,
And this same needy man must sell it me.
As I remember, this should be the house.
Being holy day, the beggar's shop is shut.
What ho, apothecary!

[59] ducats *A ducat was a small, gold coin. Forty would have been a substantial sum of money at that time.*

[60] dram *dose*
     soon-speeding gear *quickly-acting stuff*

[63] trunk *body*

[64] hasty *quick to explode*
     powder *gunpowder. (Compare the imagery at II. 6. 10. What important relationship is there?)*

[66] mortal *deadly*

[67] he *man*
     utters them *offers them for sale*

[68] bare *poverty-stricken*

[70] starveth . . . eyes *can be seen in the starved look in your eyes*

[71] Contempt . . . back *Your despicable poverty can be seen in the clothes you wear*

[74] it *i.e. the law*
     this *i.e. money*

[75] My . . . consents *My poverty makes me consent but I do so unwillingly*

[79] dispatch . . . straight *kill you instantly*

[80-2] There . . . sell *What relevance has this to the play?*

[82] poor compounds *wretched mixtures*

[84] get . . . flesh *put some flesh on*

[85] cordial *medicine – originally one that stimulated the heart*

Enter APOTHECARY

APOTHECARY   Who calls so loud?

ROMEO Come hither man. I see that thou art poor.
Hold, there is forty ducats, let me have
A dram of poison, such soon-speeding gear   60
As will disperse itself through all the veins,
That the life-weary taker may fall dead,
And that the trunk may be discharged of
    breath,
As violently as hasty powder fired
Doth hurry from the fatal cannon's womb.

APOTHECARY Such mortal drugs I have, but Mantua's
    law
Is death to any he that utters them.

ROMEO Art thou so bare and full of wretchedness,
And fear'st to die? Famine is in thy cheeks,
Need and oppression starveth in thy eyes,   70
Contempt and beggary hangs upon thy back.
The world is not thy friend, nor the world's
    law,
The world affords no law to make thee rich;
Then be not poor, but break it, and take this.

APOTHECARY My poverty but not my will consents.

ROMEO I pay thy poverty and not thy will.

APOTHECARY Put this in any liquid thing you will
And drink it off, and if you had the strength
Of twenty men, it would dispatch you straight.

ROMEO There is thy gold, worse poison to men's souls, 80
Doing more murder in this loathsome world,
Than these poor compounds that thou mayst
    not sell.
I sell thee poison, thou hast sold me none.
Farewell, buy food, and get thyself in flesh.
Come cordial, and not poison, go with me
To Juliet's grave, for there must I use thee.

                                        [*Exeunt*

ACT FIVE, scene 2

This scene serves a double purpose – it explains to the Friar and the audience what has gone wrong, and it gives time for Romeo to get from Mantua to the Capulets' tomb. Chance has interfered with the Friar's letter but it could be argued that it is as much Romeo's impulsiveness which precipitates the tragedy.

[1] brother   *i.e. brother friar*

[4] if . . . writ   *if he has written down his thoughts*

[5] bare-foot   *Franciscans travelled bare-foot.*

[6] order   *religious order*
associate   *accompany. Friars usually travelled in pairs.*

[8] searchers . . . town   *health officers appointed to view dead bodies and ascertain the cause of death*

[10] infectious pestilence   *plague*

[11] Sealed . . . forth   *It was a common practice during the plague to seal up houses where the disease was thought to be. This ensured that the occupants were kept in quarantine.*

[12] stayed   *stopped*

[13] bare   *carried*

[17] brotherhood   *religious order*

[18] nice   *trivial*
charge   *importance*

[19] dear import   *great importance*
neglecting it   *failure to deliver it*

[20] danger   *harm*

[21] crow   *crowbar*
straight   *immediately*

[25] beshrew   *blame*

[26] accidents   *happenings*

Scene 2. *Enter* FRIAR JOHN

FRIAR JOHN Holy Franciscan friar, brother, ho!

Enter FRIAR LAWRENCE

FRIAR LAWRENCE This same should be the voice of
      Friar John.
      Welcome from Mantua. What says Romeo?
      Or if his mind be writ, give me his letter.
FRIAR JOHN Going to find a bare-foot brother out,
      One of our order, to associate me,
      Here in this city visiting the sick,
      And finding him, the searchers of the town,
      Suspecting that we both were in a house
      Where the infectious pestilence did reign,   10
      Sealed up the doors, and would not let us
        forth,
      So that my speed to Mantua there was stayed.
FRIAR LAWRENCE Who bare my letter then to Romeo?
FRIAR JOHN I could not send it – here it is again –
      Nor get a messenger to bring it thee,
      So fearful were they of infection.
FRIAR LAWRENCE Unhappy fortune! By my brother-
       hood,
      The letter was not nice, but full of charge,
      Of dear import; and the neglecting it
      May do much danger. Friar John, go hence,   20
      Get me an iron crow and bring it straight
      Unto my cell.
FRIAR JOHN   Brother, I'll go and bring it thee.
                             [*Exit*
FRIAR LAWRENCE Now must I to the monument alone;
      Within this three hours will fair Juliet wake.
      She will beshrew me much that Romeo
      Hath had no notice of these accidents.
      But I will write again to Mantua,

[29] closed   *shut up*

ACT FIVE, scene 3

Shakespeare moves rapidly on to the climax and quickly estab-
lishes the scene – the churchyard at night. Juliet, seemingly
dead, lies on the curtained inner stage which can be imagined to
be the Capulets' tomb. The audience expects Romeo and Juliet
to die but the death of Paris comes as a surprise and emphasises
yet again the tragic waste of young life.

[1] stand aloof   *keep at a distance*
[3] lay . . . along   *lie down at full length*
[4] hollow   *echoing*
[6] Being loose   *i.e. because the soil is loose*
[10] afraid   *By such means Shakespeare builds up the tension.*
    stand alone   *stay by myself*
[11] yet . . . adventure   *but I'll risk it*

[12] Sweet flower   *i.e. Juliet. Paris's conventional little poem (it*
is the sestet of a sonnet) is a reminder of the past and a contrast with
what is to come.

[13] canopy   *a covering suspended over a four-poster bed. Juliet's*
tomb is seen as a bed.

[14] sweet   *perfumed*
[15] wanting   *lacking*
    distilled   *extracted*
[16] obsequies   *funeral solemnities*
    keep   *observe regularly*

[20] cross   *interfere with*

And keep her at my cell till Romeo come –
Poor living corse closed in a dead man's tomb.

[*Exit*

Scene 3. *Enter* PARIS *and his* PAGE, *bearing flowers and a torch.*

PARIS Give me thy torch boy. Hence, and stand
    aloof.
    Yet put it out, for I would not be seen.
    Under yond yew trees lay thee all along,
    Holding thy ear close to the hollow ground;
    So shall no foot upon the churchyard tread,
    Being loose, unfirm with digging up of graves,
    But thou shalt hear it; whistle then to me,
    As signal that thou hear'st something approach.
    Give me those flowers. Do as I bid thee, go.
PAGE I am almost afraid to stand alone   10
    Here in the churchyard, yet I will adventure.

[*Retires*

PARIS Sweet flower, with flowers thy bridal bed I
    strew.
    O woe, thy canopy is dust and stones,
    Which with sweet water nightly I will dew,
    Or wanting that, with tears distilled by moans.
    The obsequies that I for thee will keep,
    Nightly shall be to strew thy grave and weep.

PAGE *whistles*

The boy gives warning something doth
    approach.
What cursèd foot wanders this way tonight
To cross my obsequies and true love's rite?   20
What, with a torch? Muffle me night awhile.

[*Retires*

219

[22] mattock *an agricultural implement used for digging*
wrenching-iron *crowbar*

[27] interrupt . . . course *interfere with what I have to do*

[32] In . . . employment *For an important purpose*

[33] jealous *suspicious*

[36] hungry churchyard *It is greedy for bodies. The image of food and eating is powerfully sustained in this scene.*
[37] The . . . savage-wild *The present time and my intentions are both wild and savage*
[38] More . . . far *Far more merciless*

[41] Take . . . that *Romeo, with typical generosity, gives him money.*

[43] For . . . same *In spite of what he says*

[44] his . . . doubt *I am suspicious of his intentions*
[45] maw *stomach*
womb *belly. Romeo addresses the tomb.*

Enter ROMEO *and* BALTHASAR *with a torch, a mattock, and a crow of iron*

ROMEO Give me that mattock and the wrenching-
    iron.
    Hold, take this letter. Early in the morning
    See thou deliver it to my lord and father.
    Give me the light. Upon thy life I charge
    thee,
    Whate'er thou hearest or seest, stand all
    aloof,
    And do not interrupt me in my course.
    Why I descend into this bed of death
    Is partly to behold my lady's face,
    But chiefly to take thence from her dead
    finger 30
    A precious ring, a ring that I must use
    In dear employment. Therefore hence, be
    gone.
    But if thou, jealous, dost return to pry
    In what I farther shall intend to do,
    By heaven I will tear thee joint by joint
    And strew this hungry churchyard with thy
    limbs.
    The time and my intents are savage-wild,
    More fierce and more inexorable far
    Than empty tigers or the roaring sea.
BALTHASAR I will be gone sir, and not trouble ye. 40
ROMEO So shalt thou show me friendship. Take thou
    that.
    Live and be prosperous, and farewell good
    fellow.
BALTHASAR [*Aside*] For all this same, I'll hide me here-
    about.
    His looks I fear, and his intents I doubt.
                            [*Retires*
ROMEO Thou detestable maw, thou womb of death,

[46] dearest morsel   *i.e. Juliet*

[48] in despite   *to spite you*
     more food   *i.e. his own body*

[52-3] villainous . . . bodies   *such as using parts of the bodies for working spells and black magic*
[53] apprehend   *arrest*
[54] unhallowed   *impious*
[59] youth   *Romeo does not recognise Paris in the dark. Romeo's maturity, the result of his love and suffering, is emphasised by the repeated references to Paris as a youth.*

[60] these gone   *i.e. the dead in the tomb*

[62] another sin   *i.e. the sin of killing Paris as well as the sin of committing suicide*

[65] armed . . . myself   *i.e. with the poison*

[68] conjuration   *earnest appeal. But he could mean that he is not frightened of the black magic he thinks Romeo might be engaged in.*
[69] felon   *law-breaker*
[70] have at thee   *get ready, I'm about to attack*

Gorged with the dearest morsel of the earth,
Thus I enforce thy rotten jaws to open,

[*Opens the tomb*

And in despite I'll cram thee with more food.

PARIS [*Aside*] This is that banished haughty
            Montague,
That murdered my love's cousin, with which
            grief   50
It is supposèd the fair creature died,
And here is come to do some villainous shame
To the dead bodies. I will apprehend him.
[*Aloud*] Stop thy unhallowed toil, vile Mon-
            tague.
Can vengeance be pursued further than death?
Condemnèd villain, I do apprehend thee.
Obey and go with me, for thou must die.

ROMEO I must indeed, and therefore came I hither.
Good gentle youth, tempt not a desperate man;
Fly hence and leave me; think upon these
            gone;   60
Let them affright thee. I beseech thee youth,
Put not another sin upon my head
By urging me to fury. O be gone.
By heaven, I love thee better than myself,
For I come hither armed against myself.
Stay not, be gone, live, and hereafter say,
A madman's mercy bid thee run away.

PARIS I do defy thy conjuration,
And apprehend thee for a felon here.

ROMEO Wilt thou provoke me? Then have at thee
            boy.   70

PAGE O Lord, they fight! I will go call the watch.

[*Exit*

PARIS O I am slain. If thou be merciful,
Open the tomb, lay me with Juliet.

ROMEO In faith I will. Let me peruse this face.
Mercutio's kinsman, noble County Paris!

[76–7] when ... him   *when I was so distressed that I did not listen to him*

[82] One ... book   *One whose name, like mine, has been written down in the book of bitter misfortune*

[84] lantern   *an architectural term for a turret with openings admitting light*

[86] feasting presence   *festive presence-chamber. A presence-chamber is the splendid room in which a monarch receives guests.*

[87] Death   *i.e. the dead body of Paris*
     a dead man   *Romeo refers to his own imminent death.*

[89] keepers   *either nurses or warders of condemned people*

[90] A light'ning   *i.e. a lightening of the spirit – but there could be a double-meaning with 'lightning' implying 'a flash of illumination'.*

[94–6] beauty's ... there   *'Beauty' and 'death' are seen as two armies fighting for possession of Juliet. The flag (ensign) of beauty is to be seen in the crimson of her lips and cheeks. As long as it flies there the pale flag of death cannot be raised.*

[99] cut ... twain   *ended your youthful life*
[100] his   *i.e. Romeo's own life*
[101] cousin   *i.e. Tybalt who is his relation by marriage*
[102] Why ... fair?   *The dramatic irony is very powerful. Romeo is so near to discovering the truth.*
[103] unsubstantial   *bodiless*
[104] abhorrèd   *hateful*
[105] paramour   *mistress*
[106] still   *always*

What said my man, when my betossèd soul
Did not attend him as we rode? I think
He told me Paris should have married Juliet.
Said he not so? Or did I dream it so?
Or am I mad, hearing him talk of Juliet,   80
To think it was so? O give me thy hand,
One writ with me in sour misfortune's book.
I'll bury thee in a triumphant grave.
A grave? O no, a lantern, slaughtered youth;
For here lies Juliet, and her beauty makes
This vault a feasting presence full of light.
Death, lie thou there, by a dead man interred.

Lays PARIS *in the monument*

How oft when men are at the point of death
Have they been merry, which their keepers call
A light'ning before death. O how may I   90
Call this a light'ning? O my love, my wife!
Death that hath sucked the honey of thy breath,
Hath had no power yet upon thy beauty.
Thou art not conquered; beauty's ensign yet
Is crimson in thy lips and in thy cheeks,
And death's pale flag is not advancèd there.
Tybalt, liest thou there in thy bloody sheet?
O what more favour can I do to thee
Than with that hand that cut thy youth in twain
To sunder his that was thine enemy?   100
Forgive me cousin. Ah dear Juliet,
Why art thou yet so fair? Shall I believe
That unsubstantial Death is amorous,
And that the lean abhorrèd monster keeps
Thee here in dark to be his paramour?
For fear of that, I still will stay with thee,
And never from this palace of dim night

[110] set . . . rest   *rest for ever*

[111-12] And . . . flesh   *And shake from off my body, wearied with the world, the burden laid upon it by the unkindness of the stars*

[115] A . . . Death   *an everlasting bargain with Death who finally gains possession of everything*

[116] bitter conduct   *harsh escort*
    unsavoury   *distasteful*

[117] Thou . . . pilot   *i.e. himself. About to commit suicide, he sees himself as a captain who deliberately wrecks his ship (bark) on the rocks.*

[121] speed   *Often glossed as 'aid' or 'protector' but the meaning 'haste' – i.e. 'May Saint Francis help me to reach the tomb quickly' – adds powerfully to the irony. It is already too late and the audience remembers the Friar's 'Wisely and slow. They stumble that run fast'* (*II. 3. 94*).

[122] stumbled   *To stumble was regarded as a bad omen.*

[124] Bliss . . . you   *God bless you*

[125] vainly   *in vain*

Depart again. Here, here will I remain
With worms that are thy chamber-maids. O
    here
Will I set up my everlasting rest,   110
And shake the yoke of inauspicious stars
From this world-wearied flesh. Eyes, look your
    last.
Arms, take your last embrace. And lips, O you,
The doors of breath, seal with a righteous kiss
A dateless bargain to engrossing Death.
[*Takes out the poison*] Come bitter conduct,
    come unsavoury guide,
Thou desperate pilot, now at once run on
The dashing rocks thy sea-sick weary bark.
Here's to my love! [*Drinks*] O true apothe-
    cary!
Thy drugs are quick. Thus with a kiss I
    die.   120

Enter FRIAR LAWRENCE, *with lantern, crow and spade*

FRIAR LAWRENCE Saint Francis be my speed. How oft
    tonight
    Have my old feet stumbled at graves. Who's
    there?
BALTHASAR Here's one, a friend, and one that knows
    you well.
FRIAR LAWRENCE Bliss be upon you. Tell me, good
    my friend,
    What torch is yond, that vainly lends his light
    To grubs and eyeless skulls? As I discern,
    It burneth in the Capels' monument.
BALTHASAR It doth so holy sir, and there's my master,
    One that you love.
FRIAR LAWRENCE   Who is it?
BALTHASAR   Romeo.
FRIAR LAWRENCE How long hath he been there?

[132] My . . . hence *My master believes that I have gone away from here*

[136] ill unthrifty *evil unfortunate*
[137-9] As . . . him *Balthasar may be confused or may be pretending to be so.*

[142] masterless *ownerless, abandoned*
[143] discoloured *stained*

[145] unkind *unnatural*

[148] comfortable *comforting. Juliet is doomed not to find comfort. Compare her appeal to the Nurse at III. 5. 213.*
[152] contagion *poisonous influence*
   unnatural *drugged (?)*
[153] greater power *i.e. God. Compare this speech of the Friar's with the one he made at the supposed death of Juliet, IV. 5. 65-83.*
   contradict *oppose*
[154] thwarted our intents *frustrated our intentions*
[155] in thy bosom *Romeo is lying alongside Juliet but she has not yet seen him.*
[156] dispose of thee *place you*
[157] sisterhood *a religious society of women. The Friar's inadequacy in this crisis is illustrated by this ironic proposal.*

228

BALTHASAR   Full half an hour. 130
FRIAR LAWRENCE Go with me to the vault.
BALTHASAR   I dare not sir.
    My master knows not but I am gone hence,
    And fearfully did menace me with death
    If I did stay to look on his intents.
FRIAR LAWRENCE Stay then; I'll go alone. Fear comes
    upon me.
    O much I fear some ill unthrifty thing.
BALTHASAR As I did sleep under this yew tree here,
    I dreamt my master and another fought,
    And that my master slew him.
FRIAR LAWRENCE   Romeo!
    Alack, alack, what blood is this which stains   140
    The stony entrance of this sepulchre?
    What mean these masterless and gory swords
    To lie discoloured by this place of peace?

Enters the tom

    Romeo! O, pale! Who else! What,
        Paris too?
    And steeped in blood? Ah what an unkind
        hour
    Is guilty of this lamentable chance!
    The lady stirs.
JULIET O comfortable friar, where is my lord?
    I do remember well where I should be,
    And there I am. Where is my Romeo?   150
FRIAR LAWRENCE I hear some noise. Lady, come from
    that nest
    Of death, contagion, and unnatural sleep.
    A greater power than we can contradict
    Hath thwarted our intents. Come, come away.
    Thy husband in thy bosom there lies dead;
    And Paris too. Come I'll dispose of thee
    Among a sisterhood of holy nuns.

[161] A cup   *Romeo must have poured the poison out of the phial before drinking it.*

closed   *enclosed*

[162] timeless   *untimely*

[163] churl   *Affectionately she calls Romeo 'mean' because he has not left any poison for her.*

[165] Haply   *Perhaps*

[166] make . . . restorative   *Paradoxically, she thinks the poison on Romeo's lips will restore him to her in death.*

[168] happy   *because it is fortunately at hand and will restore her to Romeo*

[169] This   *i.e. her bosom*

rest   *This is the First Quarto reading. The Second Quarto has 'rust' which with its suggestion of the colour of blood has some attraction, but 'rest' with its association with the sleep of death and with Romeo's 'everlasting rest' has perhaps more to support it. Which do you prefer?*

[172] attach   *arrest*

[175] two days   *Juliet was buried on Wednesday. It is now late on Thursday night.*

[177] Raise up   *Rouse*

some others   *others of you*

[178] woes   *pitiful objects*

[179] ground   *cause – as opposed to the meaning 'earth' in the previous line*

[180] without . . . descry   *discover without detailed information*

Stay not to question, for the watch is coming.
Come, go good Juliet, I dare no longer stay.

[*Exit*

JULIET Go get thee hence, for I will not away. 160
What's here? A cup closed in my true love's
hand?
Poison I see hath been his timeless end.
O churl, drunk all, and left no friendly drop
To help me after? I will kiss thy lips;
Haply some poison yet doth hang on them
To make me die with a restorative.
Thy lips are warm.

FIRST WATCHMAN [*Within*] Lead, boy. Which way?

JULIET Yea, noise? Then I'll be brief. O happy
dagger!

[*Draws Romeo's dagger*

This is thy sheath; there rest, and let me die.

[*She stabs herself*

Enter Watch, with the PAGE *of* PARIS

PAGE This is the place; there where the torch doth
burn. 170

FIRST WATCHMAN The ground is bloody. Search
about the churchyard.
Go some of you; whoe'er you find attach.

[*Exeunt some of the Watch*

Pitiful sight! Here lies the County slain,
And Juliet bleeding, warm, and newly dead,
Who here hath lain this two days buried.
Go tell the Prince, run to the Capulets,
Raise up the Montagues, some others search.

[*Exeunt others of the Watch*

We see the ground whereon these woes do
lie,
But the true ground of all these piteous woes
We cannot without circumstance descry. 180

231

[185] this . . . side   *this side of the churchyard*

[186] Stay   *Detain*

Enter the Prince   *The Prince has appeared at the beginning, the middle, and the end of the play. His carefully structured appearances provide a symmetrical and significant dramatic framework.*

[187] What . . . up . . . ?   *What unfortunate event has happened so early in the morning?*

[189] should   *can*

[193] startles in   *alarms*

[197] comes   *has come about*

[199] instruments   *tools*
       fit   *suitable*

ACT FIVE, SCENE THREE

Enter some of the Watch with BALTHASAR

SECOND WATCHMAN Here's Romeo's man; we found
    him in the churchyard.
FIRST WATCHMAN Hold him in safety till the Prince
    come hither.

Enter FRIAR LAWRENCE *with another* WATCHMAN

THIRD WATCHMAN Here is a friar that trembles, sighs,
    and weeps.
    We took this mattock and this spade from him
    As he was coming from this churchyard's side.
FIRST WATCHMAN A great suspicion! Stay the friar too.

Enter the PRINCE *and* ATTENDANTS

PRINCE What misadventure is so early up,
    That calls our person from our morning rest?

Enter CAPULET *and* LADY CAPULET

CAPULET What should it be that is so shrieked abroad?
LADY CAPULET The people in the street cry 'Romeo'; 190
    Some 'Juliet', and some 'Paris', and all run
    With open outcry toward our monument.
PRINCE What fear is this which startles in your ears?
FIRST WATCHMAN Sovereign, here lies the County
    Paris slain,
    And Romeo dead, and Juliet, dead before,
    Warm and new killed.
PRINCE Search, seek, and know how this foul murder
    comes.
FIRST WATCHMAN Here is a friar, and slaughtered
    Romeo's man,
    With instruments upon them, fit to open
    These dead men's tombs. 200

[202] mista'en *made a mistake*
his house *i.e. its sheath*
[203] Montague *Romeo*
[204] mis-sheathèd *wrongly sheathed*

[206] warns *summons*
old age *Perhaps Lady Capulet is older than she has previously admitted.*

[208] down *struck down by death*
[209] is . . . tonight *died last night. Lady Montague's concern for her son is deftly portrayed in the few lines she has in I. 1. Significantly she is the only one of the older characters to die.*

[213] thou untaught *How bad mannered of you, Romeo! This emphasises the unnaturalness of the young dying before the old.*
[215] the . . . outrage *your passionate outcry*
[216] clear . . . ambiguities *understand these uncertainties*
[217] spring *source*
[218] general . . . woes *leader of your mourning*
[219] forbear *restrain yourselves*
[220] And . . . patience *And let us master our misfortunes by the exercise of our patience*
[221] parties of suspicion *those who are suspected*
[222] greatest . . . least *under greatest suspicion but because of my age and weakness least able (to have carried out the murder)*
[224] make against *point to*
[225] impeach and purge *accuse and clear myself*
[226] Myself . . . excused *Accused by myself and found innocent by myself*
[228–68] I will . . . law *What justification is there for this long passage which appears merely to recount what the audience already knows?*
[228–9] for . . . tale *for the short time I have left to live is not as long as it would take to tell a long and tedious tale*

CAPULET O heavens! O wife, look how our daughter
    bleeds.
    This dagger hath mista'en, for lo his house
    Is empty on the back of Montague,
    And is mis-sheathèd in my daughter's bosom.
LADY CAPULET O me, this sight of death is as a bell,
    That warns my old age to a sepulchre.

Enter MONTAGUE

PRINCE Come Montague, for thou art early up
    To see thy son and heir more early down.
MONTAGUE Alas my liege, my wife is dead tonight.
    Grief of my son's exile hath stopped her
      breath.   210
    What further woe conspires against mine age?
PRINCE Look and thou shalt see.
MONTAGUE O thou untaught, what manners is in this,
    To press before thy father to a grave?
PRINCE Seal up the mouth of outrage for a while,
    Till we can clear these ambiguities,
    And know their spring, their head, their true
      descent;
    And then will I be general of your woes,
    And lead you even to death. Meantime forbear,
    And let mischance be slave to patience.   220
    Bring forth the parties of suspicion.
FRIAR LAWRENCE I am the greatest, able to do least,
    Yet most suspected, as the time and place
    Doth make against me, of this direful murder.
    And here I stand both to impeach and purge
    Myself condemnèd, and myself excused.
PRINCE Then say at once what thou dost know in this.
FRIAR LAWRENCE I will be brief, for my short date of
      breath
    Is not so long as is a tedious tale.
    Romeo, there dead, was husband to that Juliet; 230

[232] stolen   *secret*
[233] dooms-day   *day of death*

[236] You   *i.e. Capulet*
      siege of grief   *grief by which she was attacked*
[237] perforce   *by force*

[239] mean   *way*

[242] art   *i.e. his knowledge of herbs and drugs*

[244] wrought on   *produced in*

[246] as   *on*
      dire   *terrible*
[247] borrowed   *temporary*
[248] force . . . cease   *effects should wear off*

[250] stayed   *delayed*
      yesternight   *last night*
[252] prefixed   *prearranged*

[254] closely   *secretly*

[260] work of heaven.   *Religion increasingly takes the place of astrology as the play nears its end.*

And she, there dead, that Romeo's faithful
   wife.
I married them, and their stolen marriage-day
Was Tybalt's dooms-day, whose untimely death
Banished the new-made bridegroom from this
   city;
For whom, and not for Tybalt, Juliet pined.
You, to remove that siege of grief from her,
Betrothed, and would have married her
   perforce
To County Paris. Then comes she to me,
And, with wild looks, bid me devise some
   mean
To rid her from this second marriage,   240
Or in my cell there would she kill herself.
Then gave I her, so tutored by my art,
A sleeping potion, which so took effect
As I intended, for it wrought on her
The form of death. Meantime I writ to Romeo,
That he should hither come as this dire night
To help to take her from her borrowed grave,
Being the time the potion's force should cease.
But he which bore my letter, Friar John,
Was stayed by accident, and yesternight   250
Returned my letter back. Then all alone
At the prefixed hour of her waking,
Came I to take her from her kindred's vault,
Meaning to keep her closely at my cell
Till I conveniently could send to Romeo.
But when I came, some minute ere the time
Of her awakening, here untimely lay
The noble Paris and true Romeo dead.
She wakes, and I entreated her come forth,
And bear this work of heaven with patience; 260
But then a noise did scare me from the tomb,
And she, too desperate, would not go with me,
But, as it seems, did violence on herself.

[265] privy   *a sharer in the secret*
      aught   *anything*
[267] his   *its*

[269] still   *always*

[272] in post   *at top speed*

[275] going   *as he went*

[278] raised   *gave the alarm to*
[279] made . . . master   *was your master doing*

[282] Anon   *Very soon*
[283] by and by   *immediately*
      drew   *i.e. drew his sword*
[285] make good   *confirm*

[288] therewithal   *therewith, i.e. with the poison*
[291] scourge . . . hate   *dreadful punishment has resulted from your hatred*
[292] kill . . . love   *kill your children through their love for each other. Again we have the juxtaposition of love and hate.*
[293] winking . . . discords   *closing my eyes to your quarrels*
[294] brace   *i.e. Mercutio and Paris. The failure of the ruler to keep order is an important theme of Shakespeare's history plays.*

All this I know, and to the marriage
Her Nurse is privy; and if aught in this
Miscarried by my fault, let my old life
Be sacrificed, some hour before his time,
Unto the rigour of severest law.

PRINCE We still have known thee for a holy man.
Where's Romeo's man? What can he say to
this?   270

BALTHASAR I brought my master news of Juliet's
death,
And then in post he came from Mantua
To this same place, to this same monument.
This letter he early bid me give his father,
And threatened me with death, going in the
vault,
If I departed not, and left him there.

PRINCE Give me the letter, I will look on it.
Where is the County's page, that raised the
Watch?
Sirrah, what made your master in this place?

PAGE He came with flowers to strew his lady's
grave,   280
And bid me stand aloof, and so I did.
Anon comes one with light to ope the tomb,
And by and by my master drew on him,
And then I ran away to call the Watch.

PRINCE This letter doth make good the friar's words,
Their course of love, the tidings of her death.
And here he writes that he did buy a poison
Of a poor pothecary, and therewithal
Came to this vault to die and lie with Juliet.
Where be these enemies? Capulet, Montague, 290
See what a scourge is laid upon your hate,
That heaven finds means to kill your joys with
love.
And I for winking at your discords too
Have lost a brace of kinsmen; all are punished.

[296–7] This . . . demand *This handshake of reconciliation is the only marriage settlement that I, as Juliet's father, can ask for. There is a pun on 'jointure' in the sense of joining hands.*

[299] whiles *as long as*
[300] no figure . . . set *no statue be valued as highly*

[302] Romeo's *i.e. Romeo's statue*
[303] Poor sacrifices *Unfortunate victims*
[304] glooming *gloomy*

CAPULET O brother Montague, give me thy hand.
   This is my daughter's jointure, for no more
   Can I demand.
MONTAGUE   But I can give thee more.
   For I will raise her statue in pure gold,
   That whiles Verona by that name is known,
   There shall no figure at such rate be set   300
   As that of true and faithful Juliet.
CAPULET As rich shall Romeo's by his lady's lie,
   Poor sacrifices of our enmity.
PRINCE A glooming peace this morning with it brings;
   The sun for sorrow will not show his head.
   Go hence to have more talk of these sad things;
   Some shall be pardoned, and some punishèd.
   For never was a story of more woe
   Than this of Juliet and her Romeo.
           [Exeunt

Also produced by Macmillan

Shakespeare Interviews

devised, written and directed by Robert Tanitch

Four tapes, each of which contains a brief introduction to one of Shakespeare's most popular plays, followed by a searching interview with the main characters in the play. The actions and motives of the characters, and the conflict and drama of their relationships are revealed through the interviewer's skilful questioning.

Shakespeare Interviews can be enjoyed both at a simple and a sophisticated level. For the student coming to Shakespeare for the first time, these tapes will be invaluable in helping him to overcome the initial language barrier. For the student of Shakespeare at CSE, O and A level who is familiar with the play which he is studying, these tapes offer a stimulating approach, and a springboard for new ideas.

Characters interviewed:
Macbeth: Macbeth, Lady Macbeth
Julius Caesar: Brutus, Cassius, Julius Caesar, Mark Antony
Hamlet: Hamlet, Ophelia, Polonius, Claudius, Gertrude
Romeo and Juliet: Romeo, Juliet, Mercutio, Friar Lawrence, the Nurse

Macbeth	open reel 333 15111 9	cassette 333 15373 1
Julius Caesar	open reel 333 15112 7	cassette 333 15375 8
Hamlet	open reel 333 15113 5	cassette 333 15376 6
Romeo and Juliet	open reel 333 15114 3	cassette 333 15377 4